MW01294194

Before Journey's End

Jabez

A MEMOIR

Copyright

Some names have been changed to protect the rights of certain individuals.

All rights reserved. This book or any portion thereof may not be reproduced or used in any manner whatsoever without the express written permission of the author, except for the use of brief quotations in critical articles or reviews. For permission, contact author at whyme@jabezdreams.com.

Before Journey's End
Copyright © 2019 by D.D.H. Green

Scripture quotations marked (NIV) are taken from the Holy Bible, New International Version®, NIV®. Copyright© 1973, 1978, 1984, 2011 by Biblica, Inc.™ Used by permission of Zondervan. All rights reserved worldwide. www.zondervan.com. The "NIV" "New International Version" are trademarks registered in the United States Patent and Trademark Office by Biblica, Inc.™

Scripture quotations marked NKJV are taken from the New King James Version®. Copyright© 1982 by Thomas Nelson. Used by permission. All rights reserved.

Scripture quotations marked KJV are taken from the King James Version. Public domain.

Cover art: R.G.
Cover design: D. Wallace

ISBN: 9781094708027

10 9 8 7 6 5 4 3 2 1

For my family

CONTENTS

Preface

If the story of my early life had a theme song, it would be *Tears of a Clown* by Smokey Robinson and The Miracles. When I was growing up, the one thing I learned to do better than anything was hide. There were things about me that I didn't understand and could not talk about to anyone because I thought people would think me weird. My life changed when I was eleven years old with a dream that I did not understand, but which turned out to be the catalyst for the incredible experiences I have had throughout my life. My journey has led to my discovering who I am and becoming comfortable with that.

Jabez is a name my mom began calling me when I was five months old. When I was growing up, I hated it and just saw it as another nickname among the list of nicknames used to tease me mercilessly. It eventually grew on me but bore no significance until, one day, God asked me, "Why did your mother call you Jabez?"

I was dumbfounded. I had no clue who Jabez was and actually thought my mother had made the name up. I knew to check the Bible only because God had mentioned it. I was not happy to find that Jabez was a man. However, after I got over that little detail, I read Jabez' prayer, and I was moved. I'm sure my mom had no clue why she had uttered the name on her lips or that as she spoke, she was blessing me with a promise.

My life has been a thrilling rollercoaster ride between the physical and the spiritual realms, which some might find fantastically horrifying. I am constantly being faced with the challenge of obeying God in all things because some of the things He requires of me are at times paradoxical. I am also faced with challenges in my marriage because while my husband is a Believer, he doesn't believe what I believe. I deal with the pain of loss, the agony of defeat and triumph over adversity.

Once when I was fed up and asked God why He was putting me through so much, He simply said, "Remember why your mother called you Jabez. This book is your ministry, but you cannot be effective if you are defective."

And so, I've learned to be grateful for a great many things—even my pain—because there are no coincidences . . . just God's plan.

This book is filled with gripping stories of spiritual warfare that will shock you, encourage you and spur you into thinking outside the realm of the obvious. I hope this book assures you that God certainly hears each and every one of us if we are willing to listen.

For those of you who hear and see things that scare you and that you don't understand, you are not alone. When I was a little girl, I used to think I was unique, but now I know that I am not. If you have been given gifts of the Holy Spirit, I hope this book will challenge you to seek God for His will in the use of those gifts.

Blessings.

"The question will be answered before it is asked."
D.S.

The Three Rings

My dreams had been like common childhood dreams: falling, running but not actually going anywhere, peeing and then realizing that I was actually in my bed—that kind of stuff. However, at age eleven, shortly after I was baptized, that all changed.

I dreamed that I was walking alone along a rugged, desolate road when I happened upon an empty cave. As I entered, an image of a man was projected onto the wall in front of me. Although I had never met God, I knew Him immediately.

Dread gripped me, instinct prompting me to run. However, transmission glitches between my brain and my feet kept me planted firm.

In a fearsome voice, God said, "I'm giving you three rings to look after."

As He spoke, three intertwined rings of differing colors appeared in my right hand. I gasped, almost dropping them.

"Do not separate them, or I will be displeased," He warned.

I gripped them tightly.

"I will be giving you instructions regarding the rings. Instructions that you are to follow to the letter. Failure to do this will have dire consequences."

Almost immediately after He said this, a deafening boom resounded outside, shaking the ground beneath my feet and dislodging myriad rocks from the walls and ceiling. Dust fell, showering me and making it next to impossible to see. I brought my free arm up to my forehead, attempting to shield my eyes. The cave rumbled as if getting ready to jettison me from its bowels. I choked on the thick air, sputtering and coughing, glancing around frantically for the exit.

Clutching the rings to my chest, I bolted outside. I pulled up short at the scene of death and destruction. A multitude of dead people in white, tattered clothing were walking by me. But it was not like a scene from a phantasmagorical zombie movie. There were no gimmicks like partly rotted flesh, no incessant hunger for fresh flesh and no Frankenstenian stomp. The scene was no less terrifying, however. I watched, barely breathing, as they meandered by, unaware of my presence.

When I woke up, I was mortified. I was on God's radar. I honestly thought that when the big moment eventually came, it would feel a whole lot different than it did. I thought about the three rings for weeks, not saying anything to anyone.

Since I was five years old, I had been most drawn to the Bible stories in which God gave premonitions to His people. I never tired of shadowing Joseph on his journey to fulfilling his phenomenal purpose. No matter what happened to him, he had a single promise made to him in two premonitory dreams. Did the hope of that promise help him cope with the unfortunate circumstances of his life? That's where Joseph and I parted company. I had no dream. I had no promise.

My parents were ultra conservative. My father ruled with an iron fist, and my mother didn't do much without his say so. We occasionally had fun moments. However, the scale was unbalanced, the weights tipping heavily on the side of fear. I walked on eggshells because I never knew when the mood in the house would change, and it changed often, and in whatever direction my father's moods swung. My mother redirected her anger at my father towards my sisters and me. She was especially cruel to me, disparaging me at the slightest opportunity, her resentment palpable. Unlike the welts and bruises my father inflicted on my body with his belt and his fist, the scars left on my psyche by my mother's tongue were far more injurious. I was made to feel like No One. I worked up the courage to ask my mother one day if she was sure she had taken the right baby from the hospital when she brought me home. I didn't dare complain to anyone outside the house, but my face read like an open book, and the story remained the same—whatever page was turned. It didn't take a genius to read what was clearly written there. However, every time I was asked the reason for my angst, my reply was always, "Nothing." I knew that embarrassing my parents would be the worst possible offense, and I did not want to find out what the sentence for that would be.

When I was seven, I took matters into my own hands and devised a plan to run away from home. I packed the essentials, like a handful of Bustas (Jamaican hard candy made from brown sugar and grated coconut), a couple coconut drops (a confection made with brown sugar and diced coconut), a pack of Bubblicious bubble gum, two Hostess cakes, a bulla cake (kind of like a big, round gingerbread cakey cookie), a bar of Highgate chocolate with rum and raisins, two or three bags of Cheez Trix (Cheetos on steroids), my doll and way less clothing than was practical. I stuffed them into a pillowcase, which I tied to the end of an old, broken broomstick. Aside from the persistent problem with the darn pillowcase's refusal to stay in place (it had looked so easy on T.V.), my plan had a major flaw. When I was through packing, I realized I had not thought about where I was going to go. I ran down the list of all my relatives and my parents' friends, and I could think of one ideal place—my mother's sister's house. She had two sons but no daughters, and I knew my cousins would be happy for a little sister—at least I hoped they would be. However, I knew deep down there was no way my aunt would keep me. Dejected, I unpacked, but not everything made it back to the pantry. For months, I felt a strong sense of hopelessness and despair. However, it occurred to me, one day, that if God was the same as He ever was, then maybe I could have a different life. I just needed a dream. And so, for years, I waited most impatiently.

While Joseph's brothers and father immediately recognized the symbolism of his dreams, I wasn't quite sure what I was to be responsible for, but I did recognize that a ring wasn't just a ring. Worse than not understanding the dream was knowing that if I displeased God in the process, I would have to face His wrath. The dead walked by me every night I closed my eyes, and I found it harder and harder to sleep. The weight of the dream became so burdensome to bear that I finally told my mother about it. While she seemed amazed, the meaning of the dream eluded her. She reminded me that upon my birth she had given me back to God, so in essence, it was not surprising that I had had such a dream. She also said that my dream was a gift from God, and I should be thankful for it. Gift? It certainly didn't feel like it. Threat or frightmare would have been more apropos. Every day that something damning did not happen, the fear clawed and gnawed at me a little less until it eventually dissipated, taking with it any thoughts of the dream.

By the time I was to enter the ninth grade, my parents sent me to an all-girls boarding school two hours from home because it was reputed to be one of the best on the island at rearing up proper ladies. While I could care less about decorum and was more than happy to talk with my mouth full, chew gum noisily and rest my elbows on the table, I was relieved to finally be away from home. The rules were stringent, but I really didn't mind because funny enough, I felt like I could finally breathe. As the months passed, though, the novelty of my new digs gradually waned, and disillusionment set in. I felt out of place and alone. God was giving me dreams but remained distant. I had no one with whom I could discuss any of what I was experiencing. One of my housemates was Emma, my sister who follows me, but I had never told her any of my dreams, and I wasn't about to start. Although she was mature and very devout, our church belonged to a group of ultra-conservative Protestant churches, so I wasn't sure how she would react. My other housemates were a bunch of eleven and twelve-year-olds with whom my most serious conversation was whether Michael Jackson was cuter than Prince.

I needed God to talk to me, but not as the God of wrath I had met in my dream. I was in desperate need of the God of everything else I believed Him to be. Each Sunday, I hopped from church to church in the town nearby, never feeling fulfilled. I looked for God, trying to find Him in everything: the smallest rustle of a leaf, the slightest brush of the wind, the softest patter of the rain, the faintest twinkle of a star, the mightiest roll of the thunder, the sweetest smile on a face. However, my favorite place to look for Him was in the vermilion of the sunset. Many evenings, I would drop what I was doing, hoping to meet Him there. I would sit on a metal rail outside my dorm and just gaze out at the vast expanse. No matter how often I did this, though, nothing changed because God was only what I imagined.

One moonlit Friday night, I sat alone on the stump of an old tree in a deeply wooded area below the quadrangle. I knew it wasn't wise, but I felt safe because the luminescence of the moon afforded me a modicum of visibility, and I could hear girls milling around in the distance. "God," I cried desperately, "I feel so all alone. I know you are everywhere, but it's like you are a gazillion miles away. Where are you?"

And, in the quiet of the woods, I heard God say, His voice soft and kind, "I am right here."

I slumped forward as I let out a huge sigh of relief. "What took you so long?" I whispered, tears slowly rolling down my cheeks. I really didn't care for an answer. I was just happy to finally meet Him in the physical realm. He was so much more than I had imagined, and I recognized exactly which God He was. I had met the God of love. And, for the first time in my life, my tears were of joy.

* * *

Years later when I started having children, as soon as they were able to understand, I told them that they should talk to God because He hears them. I told them they could ask Him for anything and talk to Him as they would a father as well as a friend. This they could do anytime and anywhere.

When Nathan, my firstborn, was almost four, he came over to me in the waiting room of the doctor's office and whispered, "Mom, do you know that I can talk to God?"

Distracted, I murmured, "Mhmm," and continued filling out paperwork.

"Mom," he said persistently patting my arm, stopping only when he had my undivided attention. "It's true. I can *really* talk to God."

"That's nice Boogsie. Go back and play," I said gently, but insistently.

He looked disappointed but didn't press the issue. His stressing of the word "really" implied more than a one-sided exchange. He was talking about conversation. A for-real conversation. I don't know why, but I had emphasized the importance of the kids' talking to God and never discussed God's replying to them. That was a noteworthy moment, and I missed the opportunity to have a conversation with my son about how awesome it was that he was hearing God speak. The significance of that moment in my own life never once crossed my mind. I didn't even ask what the conversations were about because I was a little skeptical. I thought he might have just been saying what I expected. For a long time, I forgot about what Nathan had told me, and because of my reaction to him, he didn't bring it up either.

* * *

When Christine, my second child, was about five and shortly after our family had moved into our new home in South Florida, she began to protest sleeping in her room. It was her first time sleeping alone, so I encouraged her to be brave, alluding to her big-girl status as a soon-to-be-older sister. A few months after our move, my husband Logan left on a trip to Jamaica for a few weeks, so I took to sleeping on the couch in the den.

Very early one morning, a tiny finger poked my cheek. "Mom," Christine whispered rather loudly in my ear.

I frowned, half opened my eyes and peeked at her. "Hmm?"

I closed my eyes, hoping I had imagined her there. Small hands rocked me back and forth none too gently. "Mom," Christine said. She had raised her voice several decibels.

"*Nope. Not my imagination*," I thought, reluctantly opening my eyes. "Can you please go back to sleep?" I pleaded.

"But I'm done sleeping," Christine chided quite matter-of-factly, mouth set firm.

"But I'm not," I whined, "so can you please, please, please just go back to sleep?"

With head hung and an added pout for good measure, Christine said, "Okay," hesitantly walking away. Quite pleased with myself, I sighed and comfortably settled back into the couch.

"Mom, I just saw Dad!"

Sleepily, I muttered, "Mhmm. That's nice, baby."

A few seconds ticked by. And then I was fully awake.

"What?" I asked incredulously, sitting up. "Where did you see Dad?"

She pointed to the front door, "There."

I bolted to her side, and seeing no one asked stupidly, "Where is Dad? Where did he go?"

Again, she pointed at the front door, which was bolted and chained and said, "There! He walked through the door."

My body went cold all over. My head swam, and my heart rate slowed to almost zero. I stood dumbfounded and extremely lightheaded for a few minutes, not sure what to say. I managed to choke out,

"Chrissy, you just thought you saw Dad. Okay? It's because you're sleepy."

"But—" she began, glancing again at the door.

I didn't allow her to finish. "Come on." I gently held her hand and led her back to bed. "Lie down and try to go back to sleep. Okay?" I tucked her in and kissed her forehead.

"Mom," she grasped my hand, "Can you stay with me, please?" I nodded and obliged.

Christine's fear of sleeping in her room did not abate with the passing of the week, so one evening I asked her why she was afraid. She explained that there was a man there who spoke to her without moving his lips. Concerned, I called my mom who offered to come over and sleep in Christine's room. That night, I was watching T.V. in my room when I heard a loud thud. I raced to Christine's room to find my mother sprawled on her back on the floor.

"What happened?" I yelled, grasping her elbow as she pulled herself up.

In a shaky voice, she said, "Somebody threw me off the bed."

"What? Who?"

"A man." Unsteady, she got back on the bed. "He was trying to stretch over me to get to Chrissy, and when I tried to stop him, he threw me from the bed."

We prayed for her protection and my mom slept with her until Logan returned. I asked my husband to speak to our pastor, but only under the guise of needing the house blessed because we had recently moved in. I didn't want anybody outside the family made aware of the events that had transpired. A couple of deacons and church members came to bless the house one Sunday after service, and Christine slept in her bed without complaint after that.

* * *

A few months shy of Christine's sixth birthday, *I dreamed that my family was at home relaxing. All of a sudden, a window shattered, and glass sprayed everywhere. At the same time, the light bulbs and crystals on the chandelier splintered, raining down onto the floor. Shards of glass barely missed Christine who was on the sofa. She screamed and ducked down, covering her head with her hands. It took a few seconds, but I jumped into action. As I ran towards Christine, tiles started popping up high off the floor. I grabbed her hand and dragged her into another room. When we got to that room, the same thing happened. So, I grabbed her and ran to another, but the outcome was the same.*

Frustrated, Logan yelled over the noise, "I know who is responsible for this, and I'm going to go deal with him."

He came back a short time later, shoulders slumped, looking defeated. He remained in the doorway watching helplessly while Christine and I dodged tiles.

"Who's responsible for doing this?" I yelled.

"The devil."

I paused for a split second, shocked. "What happened?" I moved as several objects flew across the room.

"He asked where I thought I was going and said he would kill me."

"What?" I yelled. "We can't stay here!"

I brushed past my husband, dragging Christine behind me. When I got outside, I was confronted by the devil. I put Christine behind me to hide her from view.

The devil taunted. "So, you think you can stop me?"

He chuckled when I didn't answer.

"Tell you what," he paused contemplatively, "I challenge you to a game. If you win, I'll leave your daughter alone."

I had to try to save my child. "Okay," I agreed. Christine ran to her dad who was standing quietly on the sidelines, and he placed his arms around her protectively.

The match went badly for me from the onset. The aim was to score points by shooting a ball through a hoop. The devil elbowed me, shoved me and pushed me down. At times, gusts of wind sent me flying backwards, I ran into invisible walls and stepped into gook that held me in place. A few times, when I got close to the hoop, it moved farther away. If I somehow managed to get near it, it would be impossible to shoot the ball because the hoop was the height of a high-rise building. The devil scored point after point, all the while laughing and jeering me. He called me weak and useless and marveled at the absurdity of my daring. It was a battle of power, will, stamina, agility and skill meant to showcase his strength and my weakness. I was losing, big.

Sweat, mingled with tears, poured down my face. I turned my eyes heavenward and raised my hands towards Heaven and shouted, "God, help me please!"

The skies opened up and a voice like thunder rolled, "That's what I've been waiting for you to do—ask Me for help."

When I looked back towards the place the devil had been standing, he was gone.

Upon waking, I immediately told Logan the dream. I somehow expected him to react strongly given the horrifying details. But, true to form, he seemed underwhelmed except for the weird look that flashed across his face, which he managed to mask quickly. His only comment as he walked out the door for work was, "I wouldn't worry about it."

A friend called later in the day to tell me that after Logan left the house, he called one of his friends to express concern that I was talking a little crazy. His friend called his wife, who then called my friend to find out if she knew what was going on with me. I could not believe what I was hearing.

Logan and I grew up in Jamaica, where duppy (ghost) stories are pretty common and are a part of Jamaican folklore culture, so what had happened to Christine when Logan was in Jamaica was not shocking to him. However, dreams of God and the devil? They were on a different level entirely. Although we had gone to church together for years, giving the appearance of a united front, there was a great divide between us. We did not see eye to eye on what was within the realm of possibilities spiritually, and nothing highlighted that more than the call Logan had made to his friend.

A few months after her sixth birthday, Christine had her first seizure. She made countless trips to the emergency room and endured a battery of tests, including MRIs, CAT scans and EEGs. At one point, she was having so many seizures that one of her neurologists suggested she be home-schooled. Every once in a while, the dream of the devil's attack on Christine breached the barriers I had erected to keep it out. However, never once did I say to Logan, "You should have taken my dream seriously." What would have been the point? I did cry to God, begging to know when relief would come, but mostly I just cried.

* * *

I wasn't spared dreams about my last child Michael either. *In one of the most significant dreams I had of him, he and I were alone when he suddenly took off running, and I after him. It took me a while to catch up and when I did, I pulled up short. He was with a stranger. The man had a plethora of loose parts that seemed beyond excessive, like bolts, screws and nuts, along with tools on the ground, and he was giving Michael instructions in fitting up a contraption. Frantic, I called out to Michael, but he ignored me. The man, however, did not. He turned his head sharply and glared at me with a look that, sans words, conveyed an unmistakable message. That message? "Back off!" I made no move to retrieve my son and remained on the sidelines, ignored, as Michael watched and listened. Engrossed.*

The dream scared me at first, but then I realized it meant something wonderful. Michael had something special to learn that I would not be able to teach him because it was beyond the scope of my understanding. That knowledge required wisdom, and true wisdom only comes from one place. Knowing Michael was not afraid gave me great comfort, but

21

I did feel a little sad that he no longer needed me. One thing was clear, and that was that I couldn't interfere with God's plan for his life.

* * *

One evening, the kids wanted to discuss some spiritual subject matter for which they needed clarity. The conversation veered into dreams, and I ended up telling them the dream about the three rings.

After listening wide-mouthed, Nathan said excitedly, "Mom, we are the three rings God gave you to take care of!"

And just like that, the dream had been interpreted. And by one of the rings.

"Wow!" I marveled. "How simple. Why didn't I see that?"

"Because it wasn't revealed to you," Christine chimed in.

I smiled, my heart warming many times over.

What I didn't tell them in that moment was that about a year after Michael was born, Logan and I retired to bed one night. I lay in bed with my eyes closed, but I wasn't asleep. I'd had trouble sleeping since I was a child, and I often spent hours counting sheep, listening to my husband breathe or watching T.V.

At some point, I felt a presence in the room and thought someone had broken into the house. However, because I had had prior experience with the supernatural, I realized quickly that the intruder wasn't a corporal being. I tried to move but found that I was pinned to the bed. Fear gripped me, and I panicked. I tried to fight, kick, twist, turn—anything. I began to pray as I felt a hand on my stomach holding me down. I wrestled, unable to cry out or open my eyes, but I could not break free. I struggled and called out to God for help until I grew exhausted. After what seemed like forever, a hand reached inside me and twisted once. Then, I was instantly free.

It took me a while, but I prayed and eventually fell asleep. When I got up, I made my way to the bathroom. And as I walked, warm liquid gushed down my legs. Startled, I shouted to my husband.

Logan bolted upright in the bed. "What happened?" he asked.

"There's warm liquid running down my legs!"

"Did you pee yourself?" he jokingly asked.

I gasped, indignant. "No. It's warm liquid like when your water breaks!"

"What?" His eyes widened. "What do you mean like when your water breaks? You'd have to be pregnant for that to happen!"

"Really? You think?" I yelled.

That conversation went on for a while longer until one of us (I won't say who) had the presence of mind to suggest we get to the emergency room. We had lost a child at six weeks.

I never told Logan what happened to me that night we lost our child. I thought of starting off by reminding him of the account in Genesis 32:22-32 of Jacob wrestling an angel, just so he would have a point of reference and be open-minded to what was possible. However, I changed my mind. If he had such a hard time with dreams, he would never be able to fathom this.

* * *

For years, I pined for the child that was lost. I wondered about her walk, her talk, her laugh, her personality, her features. I thought she would have improved our family dynamic by providing Michael with a sibling close to his age. But, would Michael have had the relationship he grew to have with his older siblings? Absolutely not. The bond meant to be forged by the three rings was preordained, and so nothing could have severed that. Although I had been tempted on occasion, I never did tell Logan the dream of the three rings. It was enough for me that the dream made sense to the kids and that I finally understood it.

God's will is absolute, and nothing happens outside of that. I had been forewarned about disobeying any of God's instructions, and my ignorance concerning the meaning of the dream didn't make me less culpable. And so, with a twist of a hand, God made it abundantly clear that there could be no fourth ring.

Perchance Not to Dream

Not long after the dream of the three rings, *I dreamed that I entered the doorway of an empty church. I stopped, transfixed at the sight of a casket below the podium. My head screamed, "leave," but my legs were not in agreement. I inched forward, all the while filled with unbridled dread. I'm not sure why I didn't leave. Normally when I sensed impending doom, I struggled awake. Upon reaching the casket, my heart stopped, and then I burst into tears as I looked down at the still, peaceful face of my favorite cousin. Carl seemed to be asleep, yet he couldn't have been because he did not stir despite my hysterical sobbing. I stood there crying for what seemed like an eternity.*

I jolted awake at the blaring of a horn. My pillow was soaking wet. It was very early in the morning, and I heard my parents rushing about to get outside to whomever was at our gate. I listened to the lamentations as my uncle delivered the news that during that night, Carl, only seventeen years old, had died in his sleep. I have three sisters—no brothers. However, I often imagined him to be. He was brilliant and popular, but most of all, he was sweet and kind. He never once treated me as the nuisance I most definitely could be. I'm sure agony has claws because indescribable pain ripped at my heart causing it to explode, not giving way to sorrow but immense shock. I didn't cry. My tears seemed to have all been expended while I slept. I said nothing to anyone, bearing the burden of the guilt I felt all on my own. I walked around in a zombie-like trance in the weeks leading up to Carl's funeral. I wanted so badly to unload the weight I carried. However, every time I attempted to, the words stuck in my craw. No time seemed the right time and no one the right person.

At the funeral, when the children's choir was called up to sing, I had to fight to take my eyes off the casket resting below me. I could not open my mouth. I glanced to my left and then to my right. All the kids were solemnly belting out the hymn, "Jewels," tremendous effort written on all their faces. Why were their voices muted as though I were submerged? Tears stung my eyes and burned paths down my cheeks en route to the cold, hard floor. Carl was never again going to be able to do anything for me, but I could do one last thing for him. I opened my mouth and soundlessly moved my lips.

I had a hard time processing my cousin's death. The only thing that was clear was that the fault rested entirely with me. If I had not dreamed it, he would still be alive. The guilt ate at my soul and birthed my lifelong struggle with insomnia. After this, I feared closing my eyes on the off chance I would have like dreams in which everybody I loved died.

* * *

It was a long time after the funeral that I told my mother about my dream and that was only because I had had another dream—this time about a close family friend. I watched as April planted a garden of white lilies outside my house and woke up with a sinking feeling that something was going to happen to someone in her family. I poured my heart out then, telling my mother about both dreams. She encouraged me to tell April about the dream concerning her, but I was apprehensive of April's response. What if she didn't believe me? Yet again, what if she did? Maybe knowing would make a difference. What difference? I was not at all certain, but I had to do something. What good was knowing if it meant doing nothing?

So, I told the dream to April. I got a reaction I had not anticipated. Chuckling. It was in no way mean-spirited and was accompanied by a hug meant to reassure me. Instead, I felt humiliated. She gave a little pep talk guaranteeing that everybody in her family would be fine and urged me not to give the dream a second thought. For weeks, April's reaction bothered me until the dream was eclipsed by—I don't remember what—but it had to have been something more irksome.

The dream didn't remain quashed, however. A few months later, I had another dream. Only, this time, there was no ambiguity. *I stood in a room that was empty, save for the casket that stood on a platform in its center. As I watched in sheer terror, the casket opened and April's sister, Janine, alighted. She was disheveled, her hair full of mud, twigs and leaves and her white dress tattered and stained with mud. As she came towards me, I awoke.*

I told no one.

A few days later, while Janine was chaperoning some school children on an outing, there was a flash flood due to heavy rains. Janine and the children abandoned the vehicle they were traveling in and tried to get to higher ground. They were walking in single file along a banking when the earth below Janine's feet crumbled. She fell several feet into the river below and was swept away.

When my mother told me what had happened, I said, "They're not going to find her alive."

Taken aback my mom asked, "Why do you say that?"

I told her about the dream, and my mom listened in shock. "Still, maybe they'll find her alive," she said, her voice full of hope.

"Uhm," I hesitated. "No, they won't. I'm sure of it. I don't know how I know, but I do."

When the news came that Janine had been found and in the same manner I had seen her in my dream, I was not at all shocked. Instead, I was overwhelmed with anger. April should have taken me seriously when I came to her with my concerns after the first dream. But then again, what good would that have done? I wondered for a long time why God had shown me what was to happen to Janine. Was it to give her a chance to change some aspect of her life? I never got an explanation, but I felt guilty that I had failed somehow. And that bothered me for a long time.

* * *

In Jamaica, many people place huge emphasis on dreams. Some people deem it an honor if someone who dies "dreams them" (appears in a dream to them) because it means that they were special to that person when he or she was alive. So, it didn't strike me as strange when some years after my grandmother's death, she "dreamed me."

I dreamed that I was inside a house with her. She didn't speak, but I knew what she was thinking. She wanted me to follow her. She turned and started walking towards the front door, and I followed. She exited, and so did I. However, she seemed to be moving way ahead of me, and I struggled to keep up. As she walked, pieces of the black dress she had on started falling off, leaving small holes from which came worms. The sky grew darker and darker as she walked through a garden of what looked like scorched flowers. After a while, I could scarcely see her. I became terrified and decided to stop.

In that week, my mom got a call that her brother had been hospitalized. She got regular updates over the phone regarding his condition, and she sounded so hopeful that I felt guilty. I told her about the dream I had had of her mother and that her brother was not going to make it. I felt bad dashing her hopes but at the same time, I wanted to lessen the blow when it did inevitably come. And it did come.

Some months after my uncle died, I dreamed that wherever I went, he was there. He looked really sad. I avoided him as much as possible until he eventually left, but only for a few weeks.

In another dream, my uncle returned to follow me around yet again. He looked distraught, but this time I knew the reason for it. When he died, he and my mom were not on the best of terms. I tried to avoid him as I did before, but it was impossible to. I was extremely unnerved by his presence and got crosser each time I went somewhere, and he showed up. The last straw was when he attempted to help my husband take a mattress into the house we were moving into.

I glared at him and said sternly, "Look, Uncle Ned, I don't need your help. You need to stop following me around."

He made no move to leave which angered me further. "As a matter of fact, don't come back! I don't ever want to see you again!"

I never saw him in another dream, which I was thrilled about. When I told my mom about the dreams, she felt bad because she had not been able to repair her relationship with her brother before he died. I encouraged her to forgive him and to lay all the hurt feelings and guilt to rest.

* * *

I had to wear a Holter monitor to check for issues with my heart after I had had a few fainting spells. One night, *I dreamed I was in a house with my grandmother. She didn't speak, but I knew what she wanted. She wanted me to follow her, and follow her I did. She headed out the front door; however, as I was about to step down onto the porch, I heard God say, "Go no further!"*

I pulled up short, frozen. My grandmother turned around. Again, she did not speak, but I understood what she asked.

"No, I'm not coming," I replied.

She looked so sad. I leaned over and kissed her cheek. "I'm sorry Grandma, but I can't come with you."

In answer to the next unspoken question, I said, "I just can't. I'm sorry."

Sadly, she turned away, and my heart broke as I watched her walk away.

When I woke up that morning, I placed the part of the monitor I needed to over the phone receiver so that a reading could be transmitted. A short while after, I got a call.

After checking that she was addressing the right person, the caller said, "I'm calling about your monitor. The readings cannot be right. They are showing that your heart stopped for some time during the night. You need to come to the hospital so that the batteries can be changed."

"But these batteries are new. I saw the nurse change them," I said, kind of annoyed because I really didn't want to have to drive back to the hospital, having been there already that week.

"Well, you're going to have to take the monitor back because, like I said, these readings could not be right."

"Okay," I agreed reluctantly. "Thanks for calling. I appreciate it," I added, not meaning a word of it.

The kids wanted to come with me, but I insisted they stay with my mom. At one point, I almost caved in to their pleadings but thought better of it. Right off the hospital exit, I had to stop for a light. As I waited, I happened to glance in the rear-view mirror and saw a big rig exit the highway. Instead of slowing, however, it came barreling down on my minivan.

"Oh my God, oh my God. It's not going to stop," I whispered.

As it got closer, I held on to the steering wheel and braced for the impact. At what seemed like the last second, a black Ford F-150 pickup truck in the lane on my right changed lanes, moving into position behind me. As soon as it did, I heard a loud boom.

I closed my eyes and said, "Oh God, oh God," over and over.

I heard a second boom and felt my minivan slide forward. It slammed into the vehicle in front of me and kept sliding. When my vehicle finally stopped moving, I opened my eyes. I was shaking so hard, I could not move. In what seemed like a blur, I saw people running. I just sat there until I heard a rap on the window. I weakly rolled the window down.

"Ma'am," an officer said, "Are you alright?"

I could only manage to shake my head.

"Do you think you can walk?"

"I think so," I replied weakly.

"Okay. You need to get out of the vehicle. Hand me your ID and keys and leave everything else," he ordered firmly.

I gave the officer what he asked for then glanced nervously at my purse. "Leave it. I'll secure your personal effects," he promised.

When I got out of the van, he instructed me to sit on a wall off to the side. As I sat there hyperventilating, tears running down my face, I felt a gentle hand on my back. I looked up and saw a woman with the sweetest face.

"Are you alright?" she asked.

When I didn't answer right away, she added, "I'm a nurse."

Those words worked their magic. I calmed a little, but my head still swam, my chest hurt, and my throat was as parched as the desert sand. "I don't know. I hit my chest against the steering wheel," I said as I reached up and tentatively touched my chest.

She rubbed my back and said softly, "Don't worry. I'm going to get you some help."

She returned with two EMTs who examined me and asked some questions before loading me into the ambulance. I was kept for a few hours of observation in the hospital, then released. I was shaken up by this experience for a long time, but I didn't talk to God about it. I'm not sure why.

I did see my grandmother in another dream, but I wasn't happy to see her. And I made it quite clear. "Grandma, what are you doing here? You shouldn't be here. Besides, I don't want to see you," I said gruffly.

I didn't walk away from her, however, curious cat that I was. I waited in anticipation. Again, she didn't speak, but I knew what she was saying. My cousin Ryan was sick. She promptly burst into tears. I made no move to comfort her.

"Okay," I said, "But you have to leave."

She stayed rooted, sobbing uncontrollably.

"Fine," I said, impatient and very much annoyed. "I'll leave." And I just walked away and left her there.

That morning, I called my mother and asked her about Ryan, and she said he was in the hospital in the intensive care unit. I actually felt bad for having spoken to my grandmother so harshly.

* * *

As a child, I had heard that dreams of certain objects and animals signified happenings like pregnancy, death, birth, betrayal, travels, prosperity, etc. I never gave credence to these beliefs, chalking them up to mere superstition. However, after a few of my dreams came true, my mom and one of my sisters would call me if they had a bad feeling or bad dream to see if I had had one. If I didn't, then they could breathe easy. I never thought twice about indulging them because I felt honor bound to let them know. After all, what's the harm in helping my family?

On one of our visits to Jamaica, the kids and I went to spend a night at my in-law's house. As we got ready for bed, my sister-in-law Colette gave me a pillow, which she said was her nephew's favorite. Her nephew Rory had died at nineteen years old, and the cause of death was undetermined. That left many unanswered questions as well as raw, oozing wounds. As she talked about how much she missed him, tears ran unchecked down her cheeks.

That night *I dreamed that I was standing by a fountain when a throng of people walked by as though they were all bound for the same destination. One young man stepped away from the group and walked towards me. I immediately recognized him as Colette's nephew, Rory, whom I had met only once. He did not speak; instead, he handed me a slip of paper.*

The message read: I am not alone.

As soon as I read it, he walked away and rejoined the others.

When I woke up, I couldn't wait to tell the dream, anxious to comfort Colette. She got really excited as I described what he was wearing and started tossing around things in drawers looking for his funeral program. When she couldn't locate it, she called Rory's mother to ask if she had one. Colette described the outfit I had told her Rory was wearing and asked his mom if he was wearing an outfit like that on the program. He was. Colette excitedly told Rory's mom about the dream, and as I watched her, I felt happy.

After the euphoria wore off, however, I felt conflicted because although it was culturally ingrained in me that it was a badge of honor when a dead relative "dreamed you," the Bible says we are never to communicate with the dead. Needing clarity, I sought God. What I wanted to know more than anything else was how I was able to communicate with my grandmother and two others in dreams. It's not like I had gone out of my way to consort with them. They had found me.

What God brought to my attention was that I had two types of dreams about future events. One type was of Him and the other type was not. As this was revealed to me, the differences between the two types of dreams immediately became clear: the messenger and the modus operandi. When I receive messages from angels, they always ask if I understand or if I'm in need of explanation. Even when I do tell them that I understand, they often verify by asking me if I am sure. Incidentally, they never remotely resemble anyone I know. I felt like a fool for not discerning the difference all along. I was being deceived by spirits that knew things about me and my family and resembled people who were familiar to me and others around me. These familiar spirits were actually demons who were trying to attach themselves to me by revealing "truths" that I, in turn, passed on to others.

When I expressed shock that the devil would go to such lengths, God reminded me that the devil was not only like a lion that prowls about, seeking whom he may devour (1Peter 5:8, NIV) but also a thief who comes to steal, kill and destroy (John 10:10, NIV). To keep me from fulfilling my purpose and to lead to my destruction, the devil wanted me to act in contradiction to God's will, which I did every time I delivered a message from a familiar spirit. God stopped this from happening, though, when he commanded me not to follow the familiar spirit resembling my grandmother through the door.

* * *

I realized that I had no understanding at all of the spiritual realm and the evils dwelling therein, so I decided then that whenever I got a dream, I would seek God as to its meaning. What I really wanted to ask was that I be allowed to sleep, perchance not to dream. However, I knew that was not an option. So, instead, I begged Him to help me discern when spirits were not of Him. And God heard me and answered my prayer.

No Returns, No Swapsies

I sometimes receive gifts for which I have no purpose. Whether I keep a gift or even use it is a choice. While some gifts can be returned, re-gifted or exchanged, a gift from God cannot. These are the gifts of the Spirit. Some people might not realize right away that they have been given one of these gifts. However, the gift of discerning of spirits is hard to miss or quash.

Some churches have a "meet and greet" segment during service. This is when members of the congregation sing a song like, "Let us greet somebody in Jesus' name" while they go around hugging each other or shaking hands. One Sunday, I made my way towards the back of my church, shaking hands (I'm not a big hugger). As I reached to take the outstretched hand of a woman I had never seen before, I looked into her eyes. A chill went up and down my spine as I realized that the eyes looking back at me weren't human, but were those of a demon. I don't know how I knew this as never in my life had I ever seen one. I quickly snatched my hand back before she could touch me while I continued staring at the eyes. The woman lowered her hand slowly and smirked menacingly. I spun around, almost mowing over some people while I shakily made my way back to my seat.

"Oh my God," I thought, *"What was that?"* The singing was muffled by the sound of my heart beating in my ears.

I turned around and looked, and there was the woman in her seat, smirking at me. I faced forward as my heart threatened to burst through my chest cavity.

"This is how people die of heart attacks," I thought. *"I could die right here, and no one would be the wiser."*

I tried to take some deep breaths to calm myself. I wondered if she was still looking at me.

"Don't turn around. Don't turn around," I whispered trying to coax myself out of doing what I knew I'd regret.

And then I turned around.

This went on for the entire service. As soon as service ended, I went through a set of doors that led to several back rooms—the pastor's office, bathroom, kitchen, nursery. I remained there for a while. When I thought enough time had passed, I made my way home. I told no one.

I was extremely troubled by what I had seen. But who could I tell? When I asked God to help me discern when spirits were not of Him, this wasn't what I had had in mind. I only wanted the gift to protect myself from being duped by the enemy while I slept. I did not anticipate that it would include more. Now I could see demons inhabiting others? It was so surreal. I felt like a character in a bad horror movie arc. I contemplated asking God to take the gift back, but only for a split second…or maybe two…well, maybe three. Then, I dismissed the thought. If God didn't want me to have the ability to see demons, He would not have allowed it in the first place. Who was I to ask God to take back something He had given?

* * *

That Sunday set off a series of strange happenings in the apartment we had moved into after the sale of our house. On Sundays, Logan often left before me because he played in the church band. He had to get to church early to set up equipment and run sound checks before the service started. One morning, I got up and bolted the door behind him, and as soon as I climbed into bed, a hooded figure in black walked across the foot of the bed and called me by my full name (maiden name and all). I hadn't intended on going to church that Sunday, but I readied myself in record time and found myself in service.

Several mornings during the week, after Logan left for work, the mattress behind me depressed and then an elbow poked me repeatedly in my back, nudging me to move over. I said nothing to Logan because I didn't want him involving anyone outside the family as he had done after my dream in which the devil came gunning for Christine.

After one incident, when I could finally move (I usually can't move during), I flew out of bed and ran into the living room. Two weeks of harassment was all I could endure. "God," I cried from a place deep in my belly, with my face turned up towards Heaven and my arms outstretched. "I'm tired of this. I want to go to my bed and sleep. What am I to do?"

"Call Pastor Hardy," came the reply.

That I did eagerly, but a little apprehensively.
Pastor Hardy was the associate pastor of the church we were attending, but our interactions had been so brief and rare that I wasn't sure he would remember me. He agreed to see me in his office right away . . . and I didn't even have to use Logan's name to jog his memory. I thought Pastor Hardy would think me strange when I told him about the demon that had shown itself to me during service and what was happening to me at home. However, he listened intently and then talked a little about messages, dreams and gifts, especially the gift of discerning of spirits. He also told me not to worry about the outcome of any message I delivered because the onus was on God for its accurateness. I thought he would come to my house to pray, but he prayed with me right there in his church office. When I went home, all was peace. For a while.

Months later, *I had a dream that I was walking in my neighborhood and met a little girl, not more than five or six years old. Tears were running down her face as she sobbed uncontrollably.*

"What's wrong?" I asked.

She looked up at me and sniffled, "I'm lost."

"Do you think you'd recognize your house if you saw it?" I asked.

She shrugged, "I dunno."

"Well, why don't you walk with me and then when you see your house, you can point it out to me," I suggested.

"Okay," she agreed, smiling.

As we set off, a strange feeling came over me and I thought, "Something's not right here."

The moment I thought that, the girl transformed into a repugnant beast that grew and grew until it was about seven feet tall.

Laughing maniacally, it roared, "You think you're so smart. Well, one day we will get you!"

I woke up afraid and perplexed as to what I had done to inspire this manhunt. Why me? Then I realized that there need be only one reason. I am God's. This kept me on edge for a while, but I calmed when I accepted that the battle was not mine to fight. Although I knew they were going to keep coming, I couldn't live in fear. I trusted I would have what I needed for my protection when the time came. It didn't happen overnight, but I eventually managed to file that dream away in my agglomeration of dreams.

* * *

Logan had told me before we were married that he wanted to live in Jamaica. That was not ideal for me because when I left Jamaica at sixteen years old, I was intent on living the American dream and never looking back. However, when we got married, I agreed to move back there. I felt strongly at the time that it did not matter where we lived, even if it were the remotest of jungles, because Logan was home for me

A little over a year into our marriage, I left Logan. Apparently, on the day we got married, when the minister said, "forsaking all others," Logan heard, "never forsaking others." My heart totally shattered and irreparably damaged, I returned to Florida determined never to speak to him again and to end our marriage. After many months and countless letters and telephone conversations, however, I began to reflect more on my vows instead of on Logan's actions. I had said those vows before God, and for that reason alone, they were heavily weighted. To walk out of my marriage at my first encounter with "for worse" did not make for an auspicious beginning to an avowed, everlasting love. Besides, I loved my husband, and he did say he was really, really, *really* sorry. So, I decided to give my marriage a chance, and Logan moved to Florida so that we could make a fresh start.

After spending roughly ten years in the United States, Logan decided he wanted to return to Jamaica to help his parents with the family business. I objected at first but thought about how he had moved to Florida for me, so I compromised. The transition was a rough one to make. The children had a hard time with everything, including the Patois (pat-wah), Jamaican Creole. Although Logan and I spoke Patois to each other, we spoke Standard English to the kids. They complained about the buildings, the roads, the people and most vehemently, the food. On top of that, Christine continued to have seizures, and we had to find new doctors to take over her care.

The house we were building wasn't finished, and so we had to live with Logan's parents. Their house had seven bedrooms and four and a half bathrooms, and still, it wasn't big enough. My mother-in-law and I butt heads constantly, so I tried as much as it was possible to stay out of her way. It didn't help that Logan decided we were going to attend Hope Springs Eternal Missionary Church, the same church as his parents. I felt as though I were suffocating. I needed some space, if only on a Sunday.

* * *

I was happy when I was invited to a fasting and prayer meeting at a large, notable church. I sat between the person who invited me and her friend. Shortly after the service began, a woman in a bandana came in through the side entrance near where we were seated. As she sat down in front of us, I felt a chill as the hairs on the back of my neck stood up. God told me to repeat a prayer of protection, and I recited the words over and over in my mind.

But God said, "Say them aloud." As I'm uncomfortable making loud utterances in church, I whispered the words.

The woman in the bandana turned round one way and spoke to the woman on my left and then turned around the other and spoke to the woman on my right. However, she did not look at nor speak to me. She got up several times during the meeting, shouting, "Hallelujah" or "Praise the Lord" and sometimes both. This would set off a chorus of Hallelujahs and Praise the Lords throughout the church. All the while, I whispered what God told me to say.

When it was testimony time, the woman in the bandana went to the podium and said that she was once in bondage. She said that at one time she was insane, walking naked along the streets of the town. She went on to explain some of the things she used to do. Then she said that she was there to attest to the fact that she had been delivered. The congregation started praising God for her deliverance.

And all the while I sat there thinking, *"But she hasn't been delivered. Why can't anybody see that?"*

I looked around in disbelief at the people worshipping. *"Am I the only one sensing this? Somebody? Anybody!"*

I always thought that a church was such a sacred place that a demon would dare not enter. However, that was my second encounter with a demon in church. I hadn't known what to do the first time, and I didn't know what to do this time. I'd been to a couple of churches where someone would call somebody like this woman out and make a spectacle of her. Was it right to do that? Was it right to just keep quiet?

This gift was cool in theory, but it actually wasn't cool in living color. What do you do with a gift you don't know how to use?

* * *

I didn't encounter demons only in church. I had an encounter with an old schoolmate at a party for my brother-in-law Caleb. I was downstairs, and my kids were upstairs. We were there for a while when I suddenly felt uneasy and I heard a voice say, "Go check on the kids."

I immediately dismissed it as my being overprotective, but the nagging feeling remained.

I heard again, "Go check on the kids."

Once again, I chalked up the dread I was feeling to overprotectiveness.

A third time I heard, "Go check on the kids."

This time I could not ignore it, and a sense of urgency propelled me towards the upstairs. As I climbed the stairs, I encountered a former schoolmate, whom I hadn't seen for a few years, coming down the stairs. We stopped beside each other.

"Hi," I said cheerily, happy to see her after such a long time. She didn't answer but slowly turned her head in a mechanical sort of way, her eyes locking with mine.

Several pairs of eyes stared at me. I froze for a second and thought repeatedly, *"Not her too, not her too."* Then as fear threatened to overwhelm me, I chanted, *"I'm not afraid, I'm not afraid."*

I regained my composure and said, "I'm just checking on the kids."

She stared at me and in a monotone, said, "You do that."

Then, in that same mechanical way, she slowly faced forward and continued down the stairs. With my heart thumping almost out of my chest, I raced upstairs to check on the kids. They were all okay. I was relieved. Why was she coming downstairs the same time I was going up? The demons must have sensed that I was coming. What did they want?

I told the kids to remain upstairs, and I went back to the party. I glanced around for my old schoolmate and saw her at a table. She must have felt me looking at her because she stopped mid-sentence to glare at me. I shivered. This was someone I had had a cordial relationship with. Whenever we ran into each other, we would embrace fondly and chit chat pleasantly. Whatever intended harm my appearance upstairs had thwarted, the demons were not happy. I had to ensure that they did not find themselves upstairs again. Truth be told, I would have preferred going home, but I did not want to slink away with my tail between my legs. Besides, the cake was from my favorite bakery, Heaven's Mouth-watering Delight, and every time I glanced at it, it did its job. I cringed every time I snuck a peek at my old schoolmate to find several pairs of eyes glaring at me. They would hold my gaze for a few skin-crawling seconds, and then she would abruptly turn and carry on her conversation, smiling dazzlingly. Half an hour was about all I could stand, but it afforded me time enough to come up with a plausible excuse before I hightailed it out of there, my kids in tow. Logan stayed, of course. It was his brother's birthday.

Day could not light fast enough the next morning. As soon as I thought Colette was up, I called her. I needed to let her know the real reason I had left the party. However, I was apprehensive because my former schoolmate was also her cousin. After we talked a little about the party, I hesitantly told her the story, starting with, "Boy, Colette I don't know how to tell you this, but. . ." She listened, aghast.

Then she said, "Oh my God. Would you believe that last night I could not sleep? I was restless because the house didn't feel right. It felt heavy. It got so bad that I had to walk around the house rebuking and anointing the doors and windows."

My jaw dropped, and I gasped, "What? For real?"

"Yes," she said emphatically, "and now I know why."

I was extremely relieved. What I saw was confirmed by what

Colette felt, and what she felt was confirmed by what I saw. Confirmation is a very important aspect of faith as it dispels doubt and strengthens belief and trust in God.

* * *

Around this time, I was having some personal issues, and I felt the need to talk to someone. So, I called the pastor of Hope Springs Eternal Missionary Church Pastor Ellis, and we set a date. I didn't mention it to my husband, chiefly because some of my issues involved him.

Pastor Ellis arrived at my house at the appointed time, and as we greeted each other, I heard God say, "Don't speak."

"*Okay,*" I said to God but thought to myself, "*What am I going to talk to this man about? I can't just say I don't want to talk to him after I asked him here.*"

Just then, Logan drove through the gate. I wondered why he was there and surmised Pastor must have mentioned our meeting. However, they both appeared surprised to see each other. For about an hour, the two men talked about various things, and then Pastor glanced at his watch and said he had to get going.

"I'm so sorry, Sister Jaye," he said, "We'll have to do this another time.

"It's okay," I assured him.

After he left, I asked God, "Why didn't you want me to speak?"

I got no response. I felt a little disappointed at first because I really wanted to air my grievances. I didn't want to discuss any of my problems with family members or friends and thought that Pastor would be ideal. He was affable, which put me at ease, and I didn't see what was so wrong with wanting to talk to someone. As the day went on, I gave up expecting a response. First, because one wasn't forthcoming, and second because it dawned on me that God did not owe me an explanation.

That night I got my answer in a dream. I glided from scene to scene as God showed me Pastor engaged in various activities. It was like watching a movie. I could see all that was being said and done. The scenes depicted his arrogant attitude, his uncaring demeanor, his selfish actions, and his acrimonious interactions. When I stopped moving, God said that He was displeased with Pastor whom He called by his full name.

God's displeasure with the pastor who had been commissioned to lead a flock was not something I should have kept to myself. However, I rationalized that given Pastor's disposition, it was better to not offend him.

Months later, Pastor Ellis and I were to attend the same function. I was sitting in my car waiting for the kids to finish eating when Pastor Ellis and his family pulled up behind me. After a few minutes, his wife and kids went inside. As I passed his vehicle, I tapped on the passenger side window. Pastor immediately began rolling it down. I could hear him sucking his teeth in annoyance. When the window was down far enough, he leaned over the middle console and yelled angrily, his face contorting, "What? What do you want? What are you bothering me for?"

Shocked, I leaned forward so that he could see me because while he was sitting under the lamplight and I could see him clearly, I was standing in the shadows. "I'm sorry, Pastor," I said, holding up both hands. "I was just saying hi."

He laughed nervously and said, "Sister Jaye, it's you! Sorry. I thought it was Regine."

He thought I was his wife? I couldn't believe what I was hearing. When I didn't respond, he hung his head down, shook it and sighed, "Ah, boy."

I still said nothing. He continued, "I have a deadline to meet, but I can't get a chance to do anything because of all the interruptions." He vigorously waved a stack of papers in the air. "I can't even get to go inside. I have to stay out here and see how far I can get with these."

"Okay. No problem. I'll see you inside, Pastor," I said. Then, I turned and hurried away.

After the function, he sought me out to apologize again—this time having the good sense not to make mention of his wife.

* * *

The discerning of spirits, I realized, did not only mean that I could see demons inhabiting people. It was after the incident with Pastor Ellis that I realized what that "thing" was that I had had since I was little and couldn't put a finger on. I just hadn't been expressly shown before. All the while it was just a knowing, a strong urging. As a child, wherever I went, I was guarded with people because I could sense things about them that others couldn't.

A man was invited to speak during a week of crusades at Hope Springs Eternal Missionary Church. At one point during his sermon, God told me to repeat a prayer of protection. I began to whisper the words, and the more I did, the heavier my tongue became. After a while, I had to focus extremely hard so as to remember what I was supposed to say. My thoughts were beginning to get jumbled. Chairs got toppled as the speaker ran up and down the main aisle screaming and shouting. He insisted that the musicians hold certain chords and maintain a particular drum beat. He made proclamations about many things including why the church had not experienced growth. The following Sunday, I heard the church sister who had invited him to speak lauding his insight. I shook my head and thought how sad it was that people get sucked in by spectacles that have nothing to do with the Holy Spirit but all to do with self. However, I just listened and said nothing.

* * *

It's one thing to wonder, and quite another to know for certain when things and people are altogether different than they seem. It did take a little longer than a New York minute, but I eventually grew to appreciate the gift I was at first loath to have but could neither swap nor return.

My Thorn

Complying with what God asks of me has always been hard. Because of fear of ridicule or rejection, I often failed to deliver messages I'd been given. I would sometimes refuse to go where I was told because I feared I would be unwelcomed, or I felt uneasy. When I was unsure whether to continue going to the church my husband attended, I sought God. Problem is—one shouldn't ask a question to which one doesn't really want an answer. Every time I asked God where I should go and I heard Hope Springs Eternal Missionary Church, I thought, *"Nah. I couldn't be hearing right."* I skipped service and when I did go, I went with a heavy heart, often grumbling about what a waste of time it was to have gone.

One Saturday I was home with the kids, and suddenly, excruciating pain shot down my spine all the way to my ankles. I tried to walk but could not lift my feet. I was baffled because I had made no sudden moves or lifted anything heavy. I shuffled into my bedroom and clumsily made my way on to the bed. It took me only mere seconds to recognize the pain for what it was. So, in the stillness of the room, I asked, "What do you want me to do, Lord?"

The answer was, "I want you to go to Hope Springs Eternal Missionary Church."

"But why, God?" I asked. "I don't like that church. I get nothing from the service. Besides, there are people there who do not like me and are going to fight against me. I'm really uncomfortable there."

"Go where I send you, and I will take care of the rest," came the reply.

"Send me somewhere else, God. Anywhere. I promise I'll go. Just don't ask me to go to Hope Springs!"

God asked, "Do you remember Jonah?" Then, He was gone and with him the pain.

The next day, I was in service but not really with a willing heart. God had struck fear in my heart and that fear got me out of my bed and into the church. I did what God wanted for months after that. I ministered through song, helped with youth ministry and even wrote a play for a Christmas program.

During this time, I got messages for people in the church, none of which I delivered. I kept telling myself that these things were revealed to me just so I would know because the information was on a need-to-know basis, and I needed to know. I didn't want to anger anyone and more than that, I didn't want anyone thinking I was crazy.

* * *

One Sunday, I went outside to look for my children because I had left them in the car to eat breakfast, and they were taking a while. An elderly woman, who attended service occasionally, followed me outside. I turned to say hi, but as I looked into her eyes, I realized I was looking at a demon. I wanted to look away, but I knew that I could show no fear.

I looked the demon straight in the eye, all the while chanting, *"Oh my God. Oh my God,"* in my head.

And in a gruff, gravelly, deep voice that was ostensibly speech but more of a growl, the demon said, "Your sons I see, but where's your daughter?" This from a woman who could only speak Jamaican Creole!

The few times I had spoken to her before, I had had a hard time understanding her because she spoke the basilect variety of Patois, which is very vulgar. It is what is most often spoken by people from poor socioeconomic backgrounds or people with little formal education.

My heart pounded almost out of my chest—I could actually hear it beating in my head—and my legs felt shaky. I said in the firmest voice I could muster, "Why are you looking for my children?" Then fearing I might regret having asked, I quickly added, "You don't need to know where they are."

With that, I stormed off to find my children and kept them with me the entire service. It especially bothered me that the demon had asked for Christine as the devil had targeted her before in a dream, only months before she had had her first seizure. I didn't mention the encounter to Pastor or anyone else, except members of my family. I warned them all to keep their distance from the elderly woman. Caleb was very receptive and said that he would ensure his children understood. However, Logan frowned and said that I should be careful who I told that to. I was extremely upset. If he wouldn't keep the kids away from her, then I would.

* * *

Several months later, *I had a dream that I was on a train with Christine, only she was a few months old. When we got on, it was a clear, sunny day. Every time I glanced out the window and then looked back at Christine in my arms, she had grown. By the time she was a toddler, the train was quite a distance from where we had originally embarked. As the train rumbled along, I got uneasy. The sky got darker and darker. The winds blew strong. Leaves, pieces of paper and trashcans got swept away. As the wind picked up, so did the dust. Trees bent, and street signs shook. The place looked dirty, desolate and ominous. I looked around the car and realized that we were the only ones on the train. I started screaming frantically for the driver to stop and let us off, but to no avail. I held Christine close and pulled down on an emergency lever, jumping from the speeding train into consciousness.*

What more? I was already struggling to be supermom. My boys also needed me, and at times I had to really reach emotionally to give them more than the mere minimum. This dream meant that things would get worse. And they did. Christine's medications stopped working, and she started experiencing breakthrough seizures after being seizure free for several months. When the multiple doses of Valium she was given in the ER of our local hospital didn't work, the doctors decided to give her a STAT dose of a Dilantin and Phenobarbitol drug cocktail. Minutes after receiving the drugs, she suddenly fell unconscious in the middle of reading a joke to her brother from an *Archie* comic. One minute she was laughing, and the next, she was a ragdoll.

She was rushed by ambulance to Bustamante Hospital for Children in Kingston, Jamaica's capital city. I rode in the back of the ambulance, and Logan stayed behind to look after the boys. Everything was a blur. I wasn't even bothered by the loud blares of the siren, the potholes, the deep corners, the unnatural speed of the ambulance. I just kept my eyes glued to Christine's chest, not trusting to look away for a single moment. I silently pleaded with her to open her eyes. Nothing.

Although I had a sister who lived about half an hour away, I chose to stay with Christine. The ward to which she was admitted was an open room with about fifteen beds. By most standards, the room would not be considered large—the distance between the beds just little over a night table's width. The beds were metal and had no fancy mechanisms with which to adjust their positions, and some of them had obviously gone several rounds with a paintbrush. The only nurse call button available to me was my mouth. The ward was hot and humid although the windows remained open day and night. There was no recliner, so I sat for days in a cold metal chair. At nights, I lay my head at the foot of Christine's bed just to rest my eyes a little. Although it was never my intention to fall asleep, I almost always did.

The first couple days I was mostly numb. By the third day, I started to feel desperate. By the fifth day, despair had reared its ugly head, and I had to drill deep to remain positive and trust that God would wake her. Later in the day, a two-year-old boy was admitted to the ward, and I could see from the attention he was getting that he was very ill. The boy was there only a few hours when his father hollered for the nurses. The nurses grabbed several white screens from around nearby beds and rolled them over, immediately cordoning off the boy's bed. Doctors rushed in from neighboring wards, and I could hear orders being barked. About five minutes later, I heard the deep, loud howl of agony from the boy's dad. His little boy was gone. And just like that, the thin threads of hope I was holding on to unraveled.

"No, no, no, no," I whispered as I blindly staggered through the double doors to the large veranda and slowly sank on to a bench. My daughter was going to die. I squeezed my eyes shut tight to drown out the wailing coming from inside, but it wasn't working. True, the hospital was no Joe Dimaggio's, but Christine was getting very good care. Her neurologist Dr. Judy Tapper had ordered a battery of tests and stopped by to examine her every day. Still, Christine hadn't woken up. Tears ran steadily down my face.

I felt a firm hand on my shoulder, and I opened my eyes to see a tall, strapping man hovering over me. "Are you okay?" he asked softly, his brows furrowing with concern.

I shook my head, unable to speak.

"What's wrong?" he asked gently.

I sputtered and stammered but managed to tell him my story. He listened patiently and then asked, "Do you believe in God?"

I nodded wordlessly.

He smiled warmly. "So why are you crying? There's only one thing to do about the things you can't control. Pray. And when you pray, believe that all things are possible with God regardless of how bad they may seem. No matter what the outcome, whether your daughter pulls through or not, know that God is with you, and He will see you through."

And just like that, my meltdown was over—his words a bucket of ice water thrown in my face to sober me up.

The following day, I was reading a book or playing Sudoku—I don't quite remember which—and I heard a faint whisper, "Mom."

I hesitated, afraid I had imagined it. I held my breath. Then I heard it again, "Mom."

I slowly lifted my head, and my heart skipped several beats. Christine was awake. She looked at me quizzically, "Where's Teddy?" she whispered, grinning widely when she spotted her floppy companion at her side.

No matter how bad Christine's seizures got after that, I never again felt that sense of hopelessness. When she had a good day, I thanked God for it, and when she didn't, I thanked God for seeing her through it.

* * *

A little over a year later, when Christine was about ten, *I dreamed that I was in a white, open space devoid of any structure. There were no windows or doors. Christine was with me. Suddenly, two angels appeared. One stood by Christine while the other came over to address me.*

"It's time to go," he said, moving off as though he expected me to follow.

Confused I asked, "Go where?"

"Your time is up," he said. And suddenly, his meaning became clear.

I became hysterical. With tears pouring down my face I cried, "I'm not ready!"

I looked over pleadingly at the angel beside Christine, but he just stood facing forward, stone-faced and silent.

His expression stoic, the angel before me calmly said, "I'm sorry, but your time is up."

Realizing that there was no swaying him, I said, "I need to call my husband and my boys." I grabbed my cell phone and tried to dial, but it was dead.

I looked up at the angel. "Please. Just one phone call!"

His blank expression did not change. "I'm sorry, but I do not have the authority."

I clasped my hands and brought them up under my chin. "So please ask the One who has the authority."

"Okay," he immediately agreed and left.

He returned shortly and said, "You have been granted permission." As he spoke, the phone lit up in my hand.

I dialed my husband and desperately attempted to say to him and the boys all the things that were yet unsaid. Speaking as fast as I could, I stuttered, badly tripping over my words. Then all too soon, the phone went dead.

"No!" I screamed. "I was not done. I didn't say everything I needed to say."

"I'm sorry," the angel said calmly, "but it's time to go."

Tears poured down my cheeks. "Please. Can I get more time?"

"I'm sorry. I do not have the authority."

"Just like you asked for me to use the phone, can you ask the One who has the authority to give me more time?"

He paused for a split second. My heart thumped with both hope and fear.

"Okay," he agreed and glided away.

He returned in what seemed like no time at all and said, "You have been given more time."

When I jumped up from my sleep, I knew that that was the day my daughter and I were supposed to die. Despite the angel saying we had been given more time, my stomach was in knots. I felt nervous and weak. I had always had a fear of dying, and the dream made it near impossible for me to function. I tried to talk to my husband about it, but he just said, "You'll both be fine," and just blew it off.

The kids and I set off for school via a shortcut on a very narrow, winding road. As I went around a deep corner, a feeling of foreboding overcame me, and I knew that that was the moment we were to die. My last thought was, "Oh God. I should have put Christine in the backseat."

A truck was parked in the corner, and I couldn't stop, so I swung out onto the other side of the road. Just then, an SUV traveling in the opposite direction came flying around the corner. I closed my eyes and held on tightly to the steering wheel. I heard metal scraping and crunching in the most horrific of sounds as I passed between the two vehicles. When the sounds stopped, I opened my eyes and realized that I had stopped. I couldn't breathe. I looked around in disbelief because we were still alive. As I sat there, a man ran out of a building shouting, "You hit my truck!"

"I know," I said my voice quivering. I was trying hard not to burst out bawling. "That is why I stopped." I glanced over at his truck and noticed that it had only a minor scratch. I thought most of the damage must be to my car then.

He began ranting and raving, and I just listened, too afraid to lay the blame where it belonged—right at his feet. Suddenly, he just stopped mid-sentence as if listening to someone and simply said, "Go."

My entire body was trembling so much that I couldn't move.

"Go! Before I change my mind!" he yelled.

"Oh my God. Oh my God." I kept whispering over and over as I slowly eased back onto the road.

I remember the kids talking to me the rest of the way, but I don't remember any of that conversation. When I got to their school and got out to look at the car, all that was visible was a small almost undetectable scratch on the left side passenger door. Incidentally, that's the side of the car on which Christine was sitting (the car was a righthand drive).

During the testimony portion of the service that Sunday, I got the urging to tell all that had transpired that week. Despite the enormity of it all, which I should have been enthusiastic to share, I resisted. I rationalized that this was between God and me, no one else. As I sat and tried to listen to the other testimonies, I got a second urging. Still, I resisted, this time worried about what others might think. As the testimony segment was winding down, I got a third urging. Still, I sat in my seat.

Christine, who was sitting a few seats away with her head resting on Colette's lap, came over to sit beside me. She wore a look of concern as she whispered, "Mom, you need to go testify."

I frowned. "I'm not going up there."

Christine looked at me disapprovingly and whispered crossly, "You need to tell what happened so the Lord may be magnified."

I shot up out of my seat so fast. While I could ignore the other urgings and simply pass them off as feelings, that I could not ignore. I recognized God speaking, regardless of the medium.

As I testified, I looked at the blank faces in the congregation and could not gauge whether anyone was affected. *"God, what was the point? My testimony didn't seem to make any difference,"* I thought when I got back to my seat. I felt I had made a fool of myself. I worried that at best, people would think I was making it up, and at worst, they would think I was certifiable.

The experience shook me to the core, and I sought to draw closer to God; however, I still hesitated to deliver all the messages I got, withholding the ones I deemed harsh or admonishing. It wasn't because I wanted to be willful but because I feared reproach. I cared far too much what people thought of me. I still attended church, but only when I had a mind.

* * *

About two years passed, then I started having horrible joint pains. A pharmacist friend of mine encouraged me to go to the doctor. After a battery of tests and retests, I was diagnosed with lupus. I suffered agonizing pain that would sometimes keep me in bed for weeks. I still attended service, but now I had an excuse not to go most of the times.

One day as I lay in bed, my body racked with unbearable pain, tears poured unrestrained down my face. Every inch of my body, except my teeth, hurt something fierce. It felt like I was being worked over by little men wielding sledgehammers and pickaxes. Feeling like I would die from sheer agony, I cried, "Oh God, I can't take this anymore. This is too much."

No sooner had the words left my mouth, I heard through my haze of pain, "So jump."

Astounded, I squawked, "What?"

"Jump," the voice urged. "Just open the balcony door and jump, and your pain will be over."

I snickered and said, "Really? You'll have to come better than this. Go to hell, Satan, and leave me be. There'll be no sideshow here today." Respite came shortly afterward. I simply closed my eyes and went to sleep.

* * *

One night at a crusade, a visiting pastor placed his hand on my head as I stood at the altar and said, "God has a special work for you to do."

Joy filled my heart and I thought, "*YES!*"

When I got back to my seat, I whispered, "Thank you, God. I know I'm going to be healed."

56

I really didn't expect a reply. I just expected results. I thought that I would just go for my scheduled check-up with my rheumatologist and get the news that I was healed.

Instead, I got a response that was swift and sure. "No," God said, "you're going to become complacent."

I could not believe it. I sat in that seat, eyes filled with tears, long after the service had ended and the church was almost empty. I was devastated. Colette noticed me sitting there and came over. All I could say when she asked me what was wrong was that God had just spoken to me and I could not believe what He told me.

My heart heavy, I went to several prayer meetings after that, hoping God would somehow change His mind. I poured my heart out to the small group during one meeting, and afterward, one of the ladies approached me. She took both my hands in hers and referencing 2 Corinthians 12: 9 (NIV), she said compassionately, "Sister Jabez, just as it was with Paul, God's grace is sufficient for you."

I went home to read the entire chapter. When I read verses 7 through 9, I understood why God told me no and why He had sent the church sister to remind me of Paul. Paul wrote, "Therefore, in order to keep me from becoming conceited, I was given a thorn in my flesh, messenger of Satan, to torment me. Three times I pleaded with the Lord to take it away from me. But he said to me, "My grace is sufficient for you, for my power is made perfect in weakness."

* * *

I have never asked for healing since. Every day that I'm in pain, I simply ask God for the strength to endure. My thorn keeps me humble and ever cognizant of God's grace. My long-time obsession with death is gone. I am no longer consumed with the fear of dying. My only concern now is how I'm living.

Structural Damage

I pulled the curtains back and peered out the window as I did every morning. I gasped and dropped the curtains. I raced upstairs. "Logan, there are men in our yard," I said, breathlessly.

"I know," he said calmly. "They are here to build the wall."

I frowned and asked, "What wall?"

"The retaining wall," he said, shrugging into a t-shirt. He headed downstairs and out the door without a backward glance.

Exasperated, I peered out a window. There, at the top of the incline near the beginning of the driveway, were Logan's parents Eustace and Constance. They were talking to Logan and a group of about eight men. Constance was very animated, waving her hands to and fro and pointing periodically. Eustace was more stoic, his hands folded behind his back.

"Seriously? This is crazy. What are Constance and Eustace doing here, and why didn't I know about this?" I fumed.

Old feelings bubbled to the surface. I had to go out there. This was my home. I hurriedly got dressed and marched out the front door. After a curt good morning to all present, I addressed Logan. "What's going on?"

"The crew is starting the wall today," Logan said quite casually, as if I had had prior knowledge before mere minutes ago.

I boiled, wanting to erupt, but I held myself in check and calmly asked, "So, what's the plan?"

As Constance jumped in to explain, I wanted to scream, "Who the @&%# is talking to you? I'm talking to my husband!" Instead, I tuned her out. All I heard coming from her lips was, "Blah blah. Blah blah blah."

I focused instead on Eustace, who was discussing the height of the wall with the foreman. I marched over to join them. As Eustace swung his hand up to show the foreman where he wanted the wall to stop, I interjected, "No. I want the wall higher than that." Then, I gave Logan a look that said, *"Dare say anything different."*

He looked from me to his dad and then back at me and then said to the foreman, "I agree with Jabez. The wall needs to be higher." Satisfied, I gave the foreman my instructions, excused myself and closed the front door behind me far more quietly than I intended.

* * *

I really hated feeling like I did, but it sucked from my position at the base of the totem pole. Our entire marriage was like that. Logan would discuss and finalize plans with his parents behind my back, and then I would simply be told what was to be done. Sometimes, as with the case of the wall, I wouldn't be told at all. I would just see their plans set in motion. Whenever I voiced objections, Constance used caustic putdowns to try guilt tripping me into heeling, but I was nobody's little lapdog. Implying that my lack of compliance meant I didn't love my husband stung the most, albeit it wasn't the most damaging of projectiles.

Logan's excuse for his mother's castigating me was almost always the same. "That's just how Mommy is. Apparently, you grew up in a bubble where everything was sugar-coated for you. Well, my mother is blunt. She tells it like it is, so deal with."

In an attempt to make him understand the extent of his mother's brashness, one day, I likened Constance's tongue to that of a viper's. "What the @&%# do you want me to do? She's my mother," Logan snapped, his lips curled in disdain, his voice cold and hard.

His response was like a slap to the face. I decided then that I would fight my own battles with Constance. Funny, but blunt wasn't the adjective used to describe me when I was the one dishing up a serving of tell-it-like-it-is sauce.

As the weeks went by and more and more of the wall went up, I began to see it as a blueprint for my marriage. The back retaining wall had to be built up about fifteen feet from the road just to be level with our backyard. A four-foot concrete decorative fence was then added to that. The monstrosity rivaled the two walls Logan and I were building in our marriage. My husband and his family were behind his wall, and the kids and I were behind my wall. However, I didn't blame Constance and Eustace entirely for that because the Bible didn't call for the parents to leave the man, but for the man to leave his parents. Apparently, Logan fell asleep during the "leave and cleave" portion of our wedding sermon.

Once, we were at dinner at Constance and Eustace's house, and Caleb stopped by to drop off the keys to their store (Logan and his two brothers worked in the family business). Constance told Caleb to sit and join us, and he agreed but then turned to leave the room.

"Where are you going?" Constance asked, sounding a bit annoyed.

"I'm going to go call Colette," Caleb explained.

Constance's face turned beet red. "What are you calling her for?" she asked, raising her voice.

Caleb frowned and said calmly, "To let her know I won't be home for dinner."

Constance's face contorted as she screamed, "Why do you have to call her? You don't need to call her!" She slammed both her hands down on the table and ordered, "Sit down!"

I held my breath, waiting for the volcano I knew was about to erupt. To my chagrin, Caleb took his seat without a word. I cringed inside because I could see Logan doing exactly that.

* * *

One evening, the kids and I came home to find that Christine's bicycle had been stolen from the garage. She was devastated, and I was furious.

I hugged her and said, "Don't worry Boogsie, I'll get you another bike."

Her face lit up. "Can you get me one exactly like mine?"

"I'll try," I promised, smiling to hide how I really felt.

When I was alone in my room, I blew up. "God," I shouted as I turned my eyes upturned and jerked my outstretched hands every few words to aid in emphasis and punctuation. "I. Can. Not. Believe someone would do this. Make it impossible for the person who took the bike to enjoy it. When he sits on it, let him be uncomfortable. Give him no peace. Don't let him rest until he brings the bike back." This cry was passionate, fueled by immense frustration and rage that came from a place deep inside.

Over the next couple days, I assured Christine she needn't worry about the bike, all the while stewing about having to replace it. Then one evening, a week after the bike was taken, maybe about an hour after we got home, I heard the gate rattling. I quickly went to a window and there, leaning against the gate, was my daughter's bike. It took me a while to move because I wasn't sure I was seeing right. Then, I ran out to the gate and looked up and down the street. I saw no one. I examined the bike, and it appeared to be in the same condition it had been in prior to being taken. I pushed it into the garage and called the kids to come see. Christine was ecstatic, forgetting all about the new bike she had been promised.

I had to tell someone, so I called Colette. "You're not going to believe it, but Chrissy's bike is back," I cried. "Really?" she said.

"Yes," I cried, my voice squeaky and breathy as I rattled off the details.

"You took it up?" she asked incredulously. "Why? I wouldn't do that."

"Of course I took it up," I said. "I covered it with The Blood and leaned it up in the garage, and when Chrissy's ready to ride it, I'll just wash it off."

"Okay. But still…" she said apprehensively.

I fully understood her reaction. She was thinking of Obeah (oh-bee-yah), a practice of the occult in which supernatural forces are harnessed for personal use. Many a misfortune, such as a freak accident, unexplained illness, failed venture, insanity and sudden death, is blamed on Obeah. One aspect of Obeah involves "setting something" for someone, as in putting a spell on an object that, once touched, inevitably leads to that person's downfall or demise. A lot of people are therefore leery of eating from people, accepting gifts or lending their belongings to others.

"It doesn't matter what anybody may have done to the bike. It's covered by the blood of Jesus, so no harm can come to Chrissy. What I'm really shocked about is that they actually brought it back. I really didn't expect to see the bike again. Who returns a stolen bike? It's not like we'd ever find out who took it." I rambled.

"Why are you surprised?" Colette asked. "Isn't that what you prayed for? All you need is a little faith. Our faith need not be bigger than a mustard seed to move mountains. The Bible says the fervent prayer of a righteous man availeth much, so why bother praying if you don't expect your prayer to accomplish anything? I don't understand."

I was ashamed. I didn't understand either. When the bike was taken, I didn't tell Chrissy to pray that the bike be returned. I immediately promised to get her another bike. Colette had described my rantings as prayer. That wasn't a prayer. It was a vent. But, if it were a vent, why did God respond? I had had conversations with God that I deemed just that—conversations—God and me chatting it up. But, when I prayed, I approached Him as I had been taught. I addressed Him by title, praised Him for who He was, thanked Him for what He had done, then asked for what I wanted, making sure to end with the words, "In Jesus' name I pray"—and all this from a position of submission or reverence—standing with my hands clasped and my head bowed, lying prostrate on my bed or kneeling by my bedside. Here it was that I had done none of that, yet God had still given me what I asked for. Apparently, I was misguided in my belief in what constituted prayer. The key was my being fervent, which is about being a number of things: passionate, genuine, vehement, honest, determined, intense, emotional, true.

* * *

Logan insisted Chrissy have as normal a childhood as possible. He didn't want her to feel like she was different from other kids, so we sent her to school. I, on the other hand, preferred she continue with home-schooling because while her seizures were not as bad as they were when she left the hospital, she continued to miss a lot of school. The nurse called me almost every day to pick her up, which was extremely frustrating. Christine went on the prayer lists of many churches in various countries; however, she didn't improve. She continued to suffer. Through it all, she displayed tremendous fortitude, never getting down and even encouraging me.

One night, my mother called me and said, "I was praying for your family, and God told me that you are the one who has to pray for Christine."

I immediately remembered the dream in which the devil challenged me, and I thought about what God had said. His response to my cry for help had been succinct. He had been waiting on me. No one else. But I had cried to Him countless times over the years. That was asking for help. Wasn't it?

"But I've prayed for her," I said, confused.

"Yes. But you have to be the one to lay hands on her."

I racked my brain. Hadn't I done that? I thought hard. I had taken her to the altar numerous times for various pastors to lay hands on her. But no. I had never done that myself.

"Ok," I said, "I'll do it."

That night, I laid my right hand on Christine's head and asked God to deliver her from her infirmity.

The following morning, as we were rushing around in the kitchen trying to get out of the house in time for school, I said to Christine, "Don't forget to take your meds."

"I'm not taking them," she said nonchalantly.

I spun around sharply and glared at her. "What?"

"I'm not taking them," she repeated, looking me square in the eyes.

I was exasperated. "What do you mean you're not taking your meds? You need them," I cried.

"Mom," she dragged the word out slightly just like I did sometimes when I was about to explain something the kids were having a hard time understanding or accepting. "You prayed for God to heal me, so I'm healed. And, if I'm healed, why do I need medication?"

I opened my mouth to protest but snapped it shut. She did have a point. So why did I suddenly feel like I wanted to jump out of my skin? I was anxious and scared. "Listen, Chrissy. You can't just quit your medication," I said firmly, grabbing her by the shoulders. "You need to continue taking them until your next appointment. Then, I'll talk to your doctor about weaning you. Remember how she did it when she was taking you off the steroids?"

Christine nodded.

"Well, I don't know how to safely do that," I said passionately. I hoped the distress in my voice would sway her.

Chrissy shook her head, broke loose of my grip and stepped back. "I'm not taking the medication, Mom. It doesn't matter what you say, you can't convince me."

I sighed heavily. I had no answer to that. "Okay, fine," I said, giving up and giving in. Christine was always very stubborn, and if she believed in something, she could not be swayed by anyone or anything, even if it meant she would be punished. My body went weak as I thought about how irate Logan would be if he knew I was okaying this. He would think I was being reckless, and he wouldn't be alone in his thinking.

I was pensive the entire ride to school, and as the kids walked away from the car, I remembered that I had stuck Chrissy's eyeglasses in the glove compartment. I leaned over, snatched the latch open and pulled out the glasses. "Chrissy," I yelled, holding them up.

She walked over to the front passenger door, rested her elbows on the rolled down window pane and leaned into the car. "Here," I said stretching over to hand her glasses to her.

She shook her head. "That's okay, Mom. Don't need those."

"Why not?" I asked highly annoyed.

"Because I don't need them. I've been healed. Remember?" she said, grinning widely before sauntering off.

Christine was the happiest I'd seen her in a long time. I sat in the parking lot long after she had disappeared into the school building. I'd created a monster. Then again, I hadn't created her at all. I thought about Logan. It wouldn't be hard to hide that Christine wasn't taking her medication. Logan never noticed when her meds were running low; besides, I was the one who always picked them up from the pharmacy.

I had a harder than usual time falling asleep after that day. I spent night after night creeping up to Christine's bedside to watch her sleep, holding my breath at the slightest tremor of her body, flutter of her eyelids or twitch of her mouth. I watched and waited and waited and watched for weeks to see if her seizures would return. However, they never did. Her five-year ordeal was finally over.

Furthermore, when I took the kids for their eye exams, the ophthalmologist said that Christine, who was near-sighted, now had 20/20 vision and therefore no longer needed glasses. She also said that the pressure in Christine's eyes—which she had been monitoring for years—had not gotten any worse, so she was going to hold off on prescribing glaucoma eyedrops. Christine shot me a look of triumph that screamed, "*See, I told you.*" And I couldn't help but grin.

The immense joy I felt when I realized Christine was really healed is beyond words. However, that joy was tinged with shame and guilt. I felt like a hypocrite. I was wont to shout from any mountaintop my implicit belief that any and all things were possible with God, yet this was the second time in a short period that that belief had been put to the test, and I had failed. Jesus reprimanded Thomas for this very thing, saying, "Because you have seen Me, you have believed; blessed are those who have not seen and yet have believed" (John 20:29, NIV).

I also felt really bad about hiding what had transpired from my husband. This was something that we should have been able to rejoice about together. On the one hand, I knew all too well what it felt like to be kept in the dark; however, on the other, it would be one less thing to fight about.

* * *

My husband and I bickered every day about any and everything. Small annoyances always festered into mammoth-sized dramas—over the top and never-ending. What upset me more than anything was Logan's nonchalant attitude to the issues I perceived as problems. Talking to him often ended up being a waste of my time and energy, and any attempts to fix our problems was like trying to stop a hemorrhage with a Band-Aid.

One morning we had an argument at breakfast, and I stormed upstairs, leaving everyone at the breakfast bar. I locked myself in my bathroom and softly cried out in frustration, "God, this is so hard. You told me that when Logan makes me mad, I should say, "Lord have mercy." Well, I've been doing that, and it has changed nothing. Every day is a fight and I'm getting tired of it. I don't want to be here anymore. I just can't take anymore. God, you said you joined Logan and me together; well, you made a mistake!"

As soon as those words flew from my lips, I was mortified. "Oh my God," I cried, "I'm so sorry. You are God. You do not make mistakes. You cannot make mistakes. Please, please forgive me."

I broke into a cold sweat. "What have I done? What have I done?" I lamented, pacing back and forth. "I just blasphemed, and there is no forgiveness for that! Oh God, I'm so so sorry."

I was extremely quiet after that. I tried not to let on how disheartened I was on the drive to school. I smiled at the kids and engaged them if they spoke to me. But inside, I was dying.

Sensing that I was not quite myself, Nathan asked, "Are you okay, Mom?"

"Yeah. I'm fine," I replied but thought, *"I'm going to hell. That's what."*

"Are you sure?" Nathan asked. He was really caring and compassionate, always wanting to keep the peace, sometimes to the point of making himself miserable.

"Yeah. I'm ok." I replied, not about to discuss any of what had happened in the bathroom.

A few hours after I had dropped the kids off and was at home, a series of texts came in from Nathan, who had taken the day off from school to volunteer at the church camp office.

They read:

> *Whatever God has fixed is fixed. How long will you pretend that what He has fixed is broken? Why do you continue to doubt?*

Believe in the things He has told you. Remember Christ is the truth. Always do what is just. You are His child. He will take care of you. Remember your problems are only tests. Make sure you pass them. Ask Christ for strength.

Ask Him to forgive you and you will be forgiven. Forgive those who hurt you. Do what He says. Nothing that happens is a mistake. And remember to do His will, not your own because in the end, everything that happens is according to His will.

How can a nation divided amongst itself stand? It surely cannot! If you are Christ's, you will hear His voice. Listen to what He says carefully. The words He speaks will bring you life and save you from the jaws of death.

Floored, I read the texts about a dozen times, then called Nathan.

"Nate, where did you get this?"

"Mom," he said, his voice unsteady. "I got the urge to go outside the office and when I did, God gave me a message for you and one for Dad. I dunno. I just started typing. My fingers were going so fast, and they didn't stop until I was done."

"Oh my God!" I exclaimed. "This is crazy! You would not believe the things I said to God this morning! And then you send me this?"

"Mom, I don't know what to say. It doesn't seem real."

"Nate, this is for real," I assured him although I was in quite a bit of shock myself. "I know this is God because no one else heard what I said to Him yet this message addresses all of it."

"Wow! Really? That's crazy, Mom." Nate's voice was filled with wonder, his voice a shaky falsetto.

"I know. Isn't it? It's surreal, but it's so crazy-cool!" I cried, equally in awe.

When we got home that evening, Nathan showed me the text he had sent to his dad.

It read:

> *Do not complain about how your life should have been or wonder what your life could have been if things had happened differently. This displeases God. Instead, thank Him for what you have. Praise Him for what He has blessed you with. Ask Him for guidance and He will guide you. Seek and you shall find. Ask Him for help and He will help you, for who can stand against the God of Heaven's armies?*

It was extremely hard to concentrate for the rest of that day. However, I was no longer dismayed. The main thing that comforted me was knowing that I was forgiven for what had transpired that morning. That mattered to me more than anything else. Sure, the rest of it was remarkable, especially knowing that there is nothing that is broken that God hasn't already fixed. The realization that my lack of faith, self-control, and judgment didn't cause me to fall out of favor with God set my heart and mind at ease.

* * *

Nathan could really talk to God! That realization jolted me almost as much as the messages themselves. I wondered what else he had gotten and hadn't said. I also wondered what more was to come. I didn't have to wait very long because Nathan's newfound courage took wings.

Nathan waited a few days and then tried to talk to his dad about the text, but Logan was really closed off. He even accused Nathan of getting the message from me and not from God. Nathan felt dejected. However, I told him I was happy I had gotten mine, and assured him that despite his father's response, he had done the right thing.

What was happening with Christine and Nate was great. They both taught me that we show the strength of our faith by how well we do on our tests. And how well we do on our tests is dependent on the strength of our faith. As it is with faith, so it is with marriage. When either is built on an unsound foundation, every time there is an earthquake, there is extensive structural damage.

Close Encounter

One night, during a week of crusades, I went up to the podium to sing "Goin' up Yonder" by Walter Hawkins. I usually close my eyes when I sing because it helps to calm me so that I can really focus on the message of the song.

At some point during the song, my body began to feel light, and I felt my feet leave the ground. I began to ascend, floating upwards slowly. I continued singing, but I was having difficulty concentrating as panic engulfed me. Soon, I felt an intense heat surround me as though I were in the midst of a fire. However, I was not getting burned. Shocked, I opened my eyes and as soon as I did so, I began falling backwards. I quickly closed my eyes and I again began to ascend. As I neared the end of the song, I felt myself slowly descend and the heat dissipate.

I was afraid to open my eyes. I was shaking so badly, I was sure the congregation could see. I had to whisper, "Left foot, right foot. Left foot, right foot," over and over as I walked back to my seat.

"*Oh my God,*" I thought as I took my seat. "*What was that?*" I couldn't focus on anything else during the service.

I told my kids and Colette but no one else. I longed to be able to share my spiritual experiences with Logan, and it made me incredibly sad that I could not. All I had dared to share over the years were a few dreams which represented a tiny fraction of my spiritual experiences and encounters. While Logan and I struggled to communicate with each other, we had no trouble communicating with other people. When it came to me, Logan was tone deaf. Most of our arguments ended up with me giving up, throwing a few choice words in his direction and just walking away.

One night, however, I decided that I wasn't going to walk away. I felt that Logan was taking me for granted and was being extremely disrespectful. We were in the kitchen having tea when we started arguing. We were in each other's faces, and as I spoke, I became so impassioned, I made the mistake of poking Logan in the chest with a finger. I didn't see him move. He roughly grabbed both my upper arms and, hurtling forward, threw me off balance. I hit my hip on the peninsula, lost my balance and went down hard on the tiled kitchen floor. Logan came down on top of me, landing hard in my stomach, a knee planted on either side of my body. He screamed something in my face before getting up, but I was too stunned to move. I could not see Logan, but I knew he was in the kitchen still because I could hear his labored breathing. I was winded, and my head hurt. It took a few moments, but I eventually got to my feet.

I glared at Logan and shouted, "I can't believe you just did that. Of all the things you've done, this is the most unforgivable. I will never forgive you for this." I stormed off and left him there.

As with many of the altercations we had had, Logan simply waited a few days and just behaved as though nothing out of the ordinary had happened. He tested the waters with cheery good mornings for a couple days, then graduated to small talk, growing more emboldened with each passing day. That encounter frightened me. It was the first time Logan had put his hands on me in an act of aggression, and it had to be the last. I just wasn't sure how I was going to broach the subject because Logan expected me to treat his transgressions as water under the bridge. However, when I was the offender, Logan declared indefinite open season on me with no restrictions on frequency or time.

* * *

I didn't want to go to conventional counseling because the one attempt we had made at it hadn't worked, so I called Deacon Lowell Lovelace. I knew Lowell since I was about ten. He lived only about two miles from my childhood house. My mom did not want my sisters and me talking to Lowell because he was older. The older I got, though, I realized that my mother's objections might have been about more than Lowell's age. My mom was big on social class and breeding. She didn't know much about Lowell, nor did she like the little she had heard. When I continued talking to Lowell despite my mother's objections, she reiterated time and again that I be careful. However, she gave no concrete reasons. And then, opportunity came knocking. Lowell had gotten into a fight with a girl. He had repeatedly hit and even kicked her. When my mother was done giving her account, she looked smug because this was not hearsay. She had had a front row seat to this spectacle.

When I heard the reason Lowell had lost his temper, I could understand. When I was growing up, Jamaica was extremely conservative and homophobic, and to have it implied that you were gay was one of the worst things that could happen to a young boy. Although I didn't agree with how Lowell handled the situation, the fight did not stop me from talking to him because nobody is perfect, and everybody deserves a second chance. Besides, he was important to Logan. They called each other "brother." When we started having kids, Lowell and his wife asked us to be godparents to their kids, and we asked the same of them. I babysat for them on occasion, and sometimes they dropped my kids to school. We went to the beach together and spent many Sunday evenings hanging out.

And so, I opened the door to my marriage to someone who eventually became like a brother to me and who now called me "sis." Lowell listened objectively to both sides as we aired our grievances. I was relieved that I had a witness to the constant frustration I had had to deal with over the years. I felt vindicated each time Lowell admonished Logan, "Logan, let Jabez speak . . ." or "Logan, that's not what Jabez said . . ." Logan did not take kindly to that, accusing Lowell of taking my side. However, I thought Lowell was doing great because he did not let me off the hook either, especially when Logan complained about my use of colorful language.

Lowell leaned forward in his seat, resting his elbows on his thighs before looking me directly in the eyes. "Jabez, it doesn't matter how mad you get at Logan. He doesn't like the language you use when you address him."

I did feel ashamed that Lowell now knew I sometimes swore at my husband, but I tried to justify my actions by saying, "Yeah, I understand, but Lowell, you've never heard the way Logan talks to me. What about respect begetting respect? Logan talks down to me like I'm the dumbest person he knows. I'll be talking to the kids and Logan will start mimicking me . . . in front of the kids. Where is the respect in that? He sometimes tells me to shut up or to move from in front of him when I'm trying to talk to him. You don't talk to a dog like that."

Lowell raised his eyebrows quizzically, "Really?" he asked.

I could only nod, afraid that if I spoke, the tears would fall. Lowell looked over at Logan. "Logan, *bredrin*, you're wrong. You don't talk to your wife like that, especially in front of the kids. Regardless of what's going on between you two, the kids should be insulated." Lowell then turned his attention to me. His gaze was so intense, it threatened to pierce right through me. I had to fight not to look away. "Someone has to take the higher ground. Both of you cannot be in the gutter."

Why was he looking only at me? Wasn't he familiar with the saying, "One hand can't clap"? I looked over at Logan. He was trying to look disinterested—even bored—fidgeting with his phone or brushing imaginary dust off the arm of the sofa. However, he couldn't fool me. The deep furrowing of his brows revealed his irritation. The fact that Lowell was objecting to the way Logan was handling our problems had to be eating at Logan's core because he owned the patent on hubris. It was one of the main reasons he wanted to return to

Jamaica. He couldn't stand the dynamic of an accounting firm ranked the second largest in the world—where nobody knew of or cared who his parents were. He especially didn't fare well under female supervisors—they were incompetent, vindictive, petty and always out to destroy his credibility.

"How did it get this bad?" Lowell said, bringing me back. How much time did he have? That was a story that would take all day. However, he did not pause long enough for any of us to respond. "There should be certain things you tell yourself you'd never do to your spouse, certain lines you'd never cross, simply because it would be a source of great pain. Jabez, God expects you to respect your husband, and Logan, God expects you to love your wife. How you're treating her isn't showing her love. Any woman would be resentful of this kind of treatment, and there's nothing worse than an unhappy wife."

The tears flowed freely down my face. I never cry in front of people, and my cheeks burned from my embarrassment. I tried my best to reign in my emotions as I told Lowell the biggest issues I had. I left nothing out, including Logan's indiscretions. Logan accused me of being too quick to believe rumors and swore he wasn't physically intimate with any of the women I had mentioned. His account of the one affair he ever admitted to morphed into an incredible tale so different from the original, that all I could think was, "*Wow*." Logan talked about the financial burden he was under, especially with the mounting medical bills. He wanted me to increase my financial contribution to fifty percent of all household expenses. He also expressed displeasure that the kids did not participate in church activities as much as he would want them to. Lowell listened and gave advice, sometimes using his own marriage for example.

As the conversation wound down, Lowell was visibly upset because Logan kept misconstruing almost everything I said and was being openly hostile, "Listen, Logan, there are things you have to change if your marriage is to work. Your wife has to feel secure, which she should, because you stood before God and promised to forsake all others. So, if something even gives the appearance of impropriety, you should shun it. It's that simple. Plus, you put your hands on your wife? *Bredrin*, that should never have happened. I don't care what she did. If these things are not dealt with, and needs be, Jabez, I will stand in court and testify on your behalf."

Although our issues were far from resolved, I felt lighter having temporarily laid all my pain, resentment and frustration down. Logan was sour for a couple days, and then he came around. With the passing weeks, we eventually got to a place where we could talk and even laugh. After all, despite Logan's faults, there was much to love about him. When we weren't arguing, he was engaging, caring, funny, thoughtful, playful, affectionate and every bit the man I fell in love with.

* * *

Even with all the upheaval, I couldn't forget what had happened the night of the crusade. I thought about it constantly and asked God to explain it to me, but I got nothing. This went on for a few months until my husband came home and told me that Sister Daisy, one of the elderly members of the church, wanted to see me. I wondered what she could possibly want because we didn't speak outside of the usual Sunday morning pleasantries.

After service one Sunday, I approached her because I was waiting for her to approach me, and she hadn't. After greeting her and chit-chatting a little, I said, "Sister Daisy, Logan told me you wanted to talk to me." Her smile vanished, and she seemed a bit ill at ease.

"Yes, Sister Jaye . . . I have something to tell you . . . but I don't know how."

I was impatient. "What is it?" I coaxed.

She hemmed and hawed a little and then said, "It's about the night of the crusade."

I didn't realize until that moment that I had been holding my breath. I exhaled. I might be about to get the answers I was seeking.

"I don't know if you're going to believe me," she said and then paused.

My stomach somersaulted. "Just tell me."

Still, she hesitated.

"Nothing you say could surprise me," I said, not being entirely truthful.

"When you were up there singing," she began, and my heart galloped. "There was a bright, bright light around you. It was so bright I couldn't look straight at it."

I'm not sure what the expression on my face was, but it caused Sister Daisy to stop speaking. "Go on." I coaxed.

"Well . . . you weren't alone. There was somebody beside you."

"What?" my mouth gaped open, the hairs on the back of my neck stood up and goose bumps danced all over my arms.

"Yes, Sister Jaye. He was in white. And when you finished singing, he went out the door."

"Which door?" I asked.

"The one behind you."

Now my mind was racing a hundred miles an hour traveling back to that night. I scanned the church, my eyes resting on the door behind me. It was closed.

"It was open?" I asked, already knowing the answer but needing confirmation.

"No. It was closed."

"Ok, well if the door was closed, how did he get out the door?" I asked stupidly. By this time, my head was spinning, and I was sure I didn't even want to know the answer.

"He walked right through it," she said her voice tremoring. She had obviously been deeply affected by the experience.

79

I held my chest. "Oookay."

Sister Daisy gently touched my arm. "Sister Jaye, as soon as I saw the angel, I knew you were going to be ok. Don't worry about your sickness. God is taking care of you."

I smiled, breathing a little easier. "I know," I said raising the arm she was holding on to, locking on to hers.

"Sister Daisy, that night, I felt as though I were going up into the air as I was singing. Then, I felt like I was standing in the middle of an extremely hot fire."

I could see on her face that she had assumed I was unaware of what had happened. "My God, Sister Jaye!" Sister Daisy said, covering her mouth with her free hand.

"I couldn't see the angel, so I had no idea I wasn't alone. This is so amazing! I've been asking God what happened that night and here I have the answer."

Sister Daisy nodded, "I was so shocked, but I wasn't frightened because I knew it meant that God is with you." Then she lifted her hands towards heaven and started praising God.

I hugged her and squeezed tight, "Thanks for telling me, Sister Daisy."

I pulled back to look at her face. "You know what's amazing?"

She shook her head.

"In a church packed with people, you're the only one who witnessed what happened. That has to mean something. You should consider yourself blessed."

As we parted company, joy bubbled inside me. Faith is at the foundation of Christianity. Hebrews 11:1 defines faith as "the substance of things hoped for, the evidence of things not seen" (KJV). The company and protection of angels is something that I have believed in ever since I was little. I had to; otherwise, fear would have consumed me. To have that belief confirmed by this encounter, and for someone else to share in that experience with me was inexplicable. I could not simply forget about it or chalk it up to another weird experience I couldn't explain.

* * *

As with all things, the devil tried to muck this up for me. A few months after my experience with the angel, *I had a dream that the devil was chasing me. In an attempt to escape him, I ran into strangers' homes. I would run in through their front doors and then directly out the back, but I could never shake him.*

After running for a while, I jumped into a car parked in someone's driveway and locked the doors. But to my horror, when I looked in the rear-view mirror, there he was in the seat behind me.

In nanoseconds, his face morphed into myriad faces, all of them ominous. "No matter where you run, no matter where you hide, I will find you," he threatened.

I jumped out of my sleep, perspiring. I immediately thought of the angel that was beside me the night of the crusade. However, I was not consoled by that because he had left. Hadn't he? That thought gave rise to a level of fear I could not check. Being confronted by the devil in yet another dream was beyond petrifying. I called Pastor James, a pastor from another church who visited Hope Springs Eternal Missionary Church occasionally, and talked to him about the dream. He encouraged me to talk to God about the overwhelming fear I was feeling. And that is what I did.

Two days later, *I dreamed I was walking along a sparse road on which there wasn't much of anything except a few buildings. I saw no one along the way. After some time, I happened upon a blind woman selling her wares. She asked if I was interested in buying something from her.*

"No," I replied, hurrying by her. "Maybe another time," I added,

not wanting to be rude.

As I walked, my neck back prickled so I turned around, only to see that the blind woman was not far behind me. When I stopped, she also stopped. I quickened my steps trying to lose her, but every time I looked back, there she was.

I continued walking, and in the distance, I saw my kids standing next to a car with my husband's parents. I hurried towards them hoping that the blind woman would leave me alone. I took a deep breath, turned around and there she was. I couldn't believe it. I ignored her and turned to greet my family. She interjected, acknowledging each person by name. As she did that, I went around to the other side of the vehicle attempting to create some distance.

No sooner had I gotten to the other side of the car, there she was. She seemed to be looking directly at me although her irises were opaque, and she had no discernible pupils. Exasperated, I asked, "How is it that you seem to be able to see although you're blind?"

She slowly closed her eyes and when she opened them, her eyes were resplendent.

"The all-seeing eye," she said softly and disappeared.

I frantically scoured the area but could find her nowhere. I wanted an explanation. What did this all mean? My eyes came to rest on a dam that was miles away. On the dam stood a gargantuan man. Although I should not have been able to, I could see him clearly. As I watched, he spread his feet wide and folded his arms as he looked directly at me. His stance was one of might. I was amazed and oddly comforted by it.

* * *

That Sunday in church, I found it hard to concentrate on the happenings. As I sat in deep contemplation, God told me to open my Bible. I didn't flip through it. I opened it once, and immediately before me was Psalm 91. As I read it, I was moved that God sought to further reassure me, through Scripture, that I had nothing to fear from the enemy—no matter how close the encounter.

How I Met My Sister

For over thirty years, I had hidden all or some of myself from all who knew me. I never discussed my spiritual experiences with any of my friends, and although I had shared some of my dreams with a few family members, I had hidden other aspects of who I was from almost all of them—like my visions, my gifts and the direct messages I was getting from God. After all, how would I start such a conversation? "Oh, by the way, I see demons . . . "?

People have come into my life at various times and for various reasons. There are many people with whom I've lost contact over the years. Some I've thought of fondly. However, I've never launched a full-fledged manhunt to find and get reacquainted with anyone because, as Ecclesiastes 3 states, there is a time and a season for everything under the heavens. This includes who I happen to come in contact with and how long they remain in my life.

Because moving to Jamaica was something I did only because of Logan, I never thought there could be any real purpose to the move beyond that. I've come to realize over the years, though, that there are no coincidences or accidents. Everything happens for a reason whether it is good or bad. I consider each event a dot, which on the surface might appear unrelated. However, if I look closely enough, all the dots connect to create a big picture that tells an incredible story.

After my experience with the angel the night of the crusade, I got a niggling feeling that my time at Hope Springs Eternal Missionary Church was close to an end. This was kind of strange because I thought the encounter was a precursor for something far more dynamic. I began attending church less and less until I was going only on special occasions, which Logan was not happy about. I continued to send the kids, however.

I soon dreamed that I walked up to a huge clay pot that was sitting outside. The pot came almost to my waist and was about four feet in diameter. It was crammed pack with green sweet peppers. I was immediately drawn to some closest to me. They were lustrous and plump. However, when I reached out to pick one, I saw that the underside was covered in tiny black spots that, when looked at together, formed a large blemish. I turned over a few others and they were all the same. A voice said, "Walk away."

I walked away from the pot and headed east towards vast, open fields. I knew where to go although I had received no instructions. I kept going until I came to a large piece of land that had rows and rows of neatly planted crop extending as far as the eyes could see. The plants resembled shrubs of some sort and they were all the same height. A lone figure stood in the distance. I approached, and as I got closer, I saw that it was Jesus. I pulled up short and just stared at Him, unable to speak. He extended a hand towards me and said softly but firmly, "Come, work in my vineyard until the time of the harvest."

I jolted out of my sleep, stoked that I had seen Jesus, my heart racing for a reason other than terror. It took me a little while to come down from the euphoria. However, once I did, confusion set in. I asked, "God what are you trying to tell me? What was that? What's the pot?"

He said, "The church."

"Okay," I said, "It won't be too hard for me to walk away as I hardly go to church anyway."

I thought about what Jesus had said to me in the vineyard. Then, I thought about everyone else. "People are going to react strongly to this. Everybody will think I've backslidden," I mumbled.

"You are a part of the body of Christ," He said.

"So, what is the church?" I asked, needing an indisputable answer with which to defend myself when the evitable fight came.

"The church is every Believer and where the two or three are gathered."

I didn't need to ask who the two or three were. I knew that Bible verse well, but now I understood it. An assembly is a gathering. A gathering is an assembly. Therefore, whether Believers meet together in a structured setting, as in a church building, or in a casual setting, as in someone's home, they are gathered. As such, the requirements for assembling together, as instructed in Hebrews 10:25, are duly met.

The Church is not a building. The Church is a way of life. It is every Believer, living according to the teachings and dictates of Christ. The Church is the Body of Christ, with each member—a hand, a finger, a foot, an eye—having a specific job but working in tandem with the other members for the proper functioning of the Body as a whole (Corinthians 12:12-27, NIV).

Relief and excitement flowed in and through me. I felt on fire for whatever God had in store for me. I basked in the knowledge that I now had confirmation I had indeed been chosen for something special. I believed it when the pastor had said it the night of the crusade. So, why had Jesus shown up to extend a special invitation Himself? He could have had someone else confirm it. Maybe I was different. Maybe I was special. After all, I had been hand-picked, set apart. Matthew 22:14 states, "For many are called, but few are chosen" (NKJV). As these thoughts swirled around in my incredibly swollen head, I had to ground myself with the words Jesus spoke of John the Baptist when He said, ". . . among those born of women there has not risen anyone greater than John the Baptist; yet whoever is least in the kingdom of heaven is greater than he" (Matt 11:11, NIV). The thorn that I had been given made even more sense.

This dream marked the beginning of my journey away from the conventional and into the wilderness where I was to be deconstructed, only to be built back up again and again and again ...

* * *

It had already been roughly four years since my move to Jamaica. Michael was now six years old and had started school, despite my protestations. I was standing in the school parking lot waiting for him one afternoon when a boy came up and wordlessly stood beside me. That boy was Daniel, whose mother Abigail was Logan's high school friend. I turned to say hi to him, but he didn't speak. I tried to strike up a conversation by asking him how he was doing, but he still didn't speak. We just stood there in silence until his mom came. Over the course of several weeks, Daniel and I had quite a few one-sided conversations. I said to Logan several times that I couldn't explain it, but I would really love to work with Daniel. In Florida, I had taught remedial English Language and Reading classes to college students who were unable to pass their entrance exams due to language barriers and learning challenges. In Jamaica, I tutored primary school kids after school. I could tell just from observing Daniel's communication skills, or lack thereof, that he had special needs. Since Abigail and Logan were friends, I was hoping he would mention my desire to work with Daniel when next they spoke. However, I wasn't about to hold my breath . . . I knew Logan.

Just a few hours after my last conversation with Logan about Daniel, my cell phone rang.

"Hi, Jabez. This is Abigail."

It took me a few seconds. I only knew one Abigail, and she certainly wouldn't be calling me. But then, it couldn't be anyone else. Frowning, I asked, "Abigail? As in Webb?"

I had made my disbelief known.

A chuckle filled my ear.

"Yes."

"Oh. Hi," I said, dragging out the word hi, not quite sure what next to say. I had passed Abigail countless times in the school parking lot;

however, all she got whenever she called to me was a perfunctory wave. And I must confess that sometimes, I held my head straight as though I hadn't seen her—or waited in my car until she drove off. I always felt a little skittish whenever I saw her because Logan's mother threw her sophistication and impeccable taste in my face every chance she got. Abigail was tall and elegant and looked like a beauty queen in her designer clothes and high heels.

"I got your number from Logan," she explained as if reading my mind. "I'm calling about Daniel. This is going to sound strange, but I was so frustrated about what to do with Daniel and school that I cried out to God. He told me that Daniel should be home-schooled. His current teacher recommended a tutor for some subjects, but what I really need is someone to work on English Language. I got that the person who is to teach Daniel should have a good command of the English Language but shouldn't be too rigid. I had no idea where to turn, and because I know that only God can teach Daniel, I told Him that He would have to find the teacher. I know that what I'm going to say next might sound even stranger. But today when I dropped Daniel off and was heading home, God said, "Call Jabez. Call Logan." I was surprised that God would be directing me to you because I had no idea what you did until I called Logan, and he told me that you teach."

I didn't realize until I needed to speak that I had been holding my breath. "Really? I don't think it strange at all. I can't believe it! Just this morning I was saying to Logan that I would love to work with Daniel although I didn't understand why. I even asked him to call you. He didn't call you?"

"No," she replied.

Goosebumps danced up and down my arms as the reality of what was taking place hit me. "I home-schooled my kids for several years until Logan insisted they go to school, so I understand that conventional school doesn't work for all kids. What is the issue with Daniel? Is he autistic?"

"No. He didn't start talking until he was six and was diagnosed with delayed speech."

I had never worked with a student with delayed speech and had yet to evaluate Daniel, but the next words rolled freely off my tongue.

"I'd be happy to work with Daniel. And let me just say that none of this is strange. Daniel has come up to me several times and just stood by me. I've told Logan numerous times that I want to work with Daniel. Now you're telling me God told you to call me? This is so crazy. Well, not crazy. You know what I mean. This is really, really cool." I was rambling. Abigail laughed.

* * *

Working with Daniel, while challenging, was very fulfilling. I was in awe that each time I was concerned about how to get a concept across to him, the method would simply come to me. For the first few weeks, I did lesson plans which I had to dispense with because they were often circumvented by something God wanted me to teach Daniel. Most times his lessons came to me the night before class or just as I was about to write on the board. Sometimes the lessons had nothing to do with academics, but with social skills.

One day I wrote the topic "body language" on the board, and before I could start the lesson, Abigail came into the classroom and said, "Jaye, you know what I got? I got that you need to teach Daniel how to read body language cues."

I laughed, amazed and pointed to the board. "That's what I got too."

There were a few more incidences like these which served to confirm that I was teaching Daniel according to God's will and that Abigail did indeed call me in obedience to that will. However, the last confirmation came in the form of a dream.

I dreamed that Abigail and I got out of a car in an isolated area.

We had to walk a distance to a particular spot. When we got there, we reached up towards Heaven and papers resembling long scrolls were placed in each of our hands. On the papers were written what Daniel needed to know.

One morning, Abigail came downstairs to the classroom and said, "Don't think me strange, Jabez, but I have something to tell you. I don't know how to say it, though, because I don't want you to think that I have an ulterior motive. This has nothing to do with Daniel."

"Just tell me," I encouraged.

She struggled for a few moments more and then said, "God says that you are not to teach every student that comes to you simply because you love working with kids. Be careful of the kids you teach. Not every child that comes to you is sent by God."

I was taken aback. My mouth fell open and I thought, "*What?*" However, I kept quiet.

"Again, this has nothing to do with Daniel. I'm not saying this because I want you to teach Daniel exclusively."

She seemed really ill at ease, so I stopped her. "This is actually pretty amazing," I said, grinning widely.

I went on to tell her about the dream I had had a few years prior with the lost little girl that turned out to be a demon. Abigail's message confirmed to me that she was indeed hearing from God. It was so I wouldn't think anything she told me after that strange. I was extremely wary of people claiming to have messages for me from God because I did not want to be misled in any way.

One day Abigail said, "I need to tell you something. I have no problems."

I wanted to roll my eyes. Instead, I laughed and said sardonically, "That's good for you, Abigail, but I've plenty."

"I used to think so too," she continued patiently, "until I gave it all up. I realized that I had no control over anything. I realized that, in and of myself, I could do nothing. And so I gave it all up. I gave it all to God because He's the only one who has any control."

The first thing that came to mind was, *"fanatic"* and so I asked, "What church do you go to?"

"I don't go to church. I used to, but not anymore."

So not the answer I was expecting.

"Really? Neither do I," I replied.

So not the answer she was expecting.

I explained why I had walked away from the church. Abigail listened, intrigued. Then, she explained why she had also walked away from the church, and her story was equally as bizarre as mine. However, that's her story to tell.

* * *

Several weeks later, Abigail came to me and said, "You need to learn to forgive. If you don't forgive others, God will not forgive you. I had to call people who had wronged me and forgive them. Most people were offended because they didn't believe that they had done anything that needed forgiving. Not only that, but I had to tell them that if I'd done anything to offend them, then I was seeking their forgiveness. Now *that* they wanted to hear and were smug and deeply satisfied. One person told me not to bring any of that to her and that that was between God and me. But I couldn't let that stop me. I had to do what God required of me. You're also going to have to do that."

I wrinkled my nose and vigorously shook my head. I'd sooner die than forgive one person in particular.

"You don't understand," I protested, becoming really animated. "Some people I can forgive, but my mother-in-law has done some mean, hurtful things to me that I did not deserve, including meddling so much in my marriage that she's caused problems for my husband and me. That I don't know if I can forgive. I think it's good enough that I simply stay out of her way."

Abigail wasn't interested in the one-guest pity party I was throwing for myself.

She interjected, "That's the problem. You think you are deserving of anything. We don't deserve anything. Nobody owes you anything. Get rid of the expectations you have of others. The moment you do that, the easier it is for you to forgive. What if Jesus had focused on what mankind deserved?"

I shook my head. "This is the worst thing you could ever tell me. I hear you, but I don't know if I can do it. The worst part is having to say that I'm sorry. I haven't done anything! I've tried on countless occasions to get along with my mother-in-law, and I always end up regretting it."

She held my gaze intently, "It. Does. Not. Matter."

"But—" I protested.

She didn't allow me to continue. "If it offends someone that you are breathing, apologize for it."

Period.

End of story.

Of all the things that Abigail had told me up to that point, forgiveness was the hugest, hardest pill to swallow. I went to the only place I knew I could go without shame and judgment, and I complained profusely.

But every time I went to God, I got no relief and so I asked, "Why? Why do I still feel like this? I am praying, but I'm no closer to where I ought to be."

God said, "You go to the cross dragging your cares behind you in countless boxes tied with strings. You pray for Jesus to relieve you of your burdens. Then, you leave the cross dragging the boxes filled with your burdens behind you."

I was in an argumentative mood, and so I persisted, "But my burdens are supposed to be lifted from me at Calvary as the hymn says. I shouldn't be able to take them back."

God replied, "Casting your cares requires an action from you—

letting go."

That night, *I dreamed I was at an underground subway station. However, the only thing on the track was an old country bus. Tied with cord to the top of the bus were numerous pieces of luggage, crocus bags and boxes. All mine. The bus was so laden, that the ground beneath it gave way, and the bus began to sink. In a matter of seconds, the front of the bus was below ground level. The backend, still above ground, was barely being held up by oversized wheels. As the earth shook, more of the bus disappeared until all that was visible was my bag and pan. In a panic, I dived on to my stomach and started frantically grasping at my stuff. I only managed to grab fistfuls of cord or air. The hole opened up even further and the bus slipped a little more, but I was unrelenting. I inched my torso forward, dangling precariously over the edge of the crater, scrambling to save at least one thing.*

God could not have gotten the message across to me any simpler. I had a problem. I was a hoarder. It was painful envisioning myself on my belly and reliving the desperation I felt as I groveled, trying to hold on to my baggage. I saw the truth regarding the great lengths I often went through to hold on to old, useless stuff. Every time I talked to Colette, the conversation inevitably veered to Constance. We would talk at length about her most recent offense and then rehash the old with, "Do you remember when…" This always led to my getting mad all over again about things that happened as far back as ten years. Charles Tindley's hymn, "Leave It There," encourages leaving one's burden at the cross. That reiterates what God had said about letting go. I decided that morning that I had to change.

* * *

I worked on letting go of myriad hurt feelings, some of which were because of Logan. Prior to the dream of the loaded bus, Logan and I

Before Journey's End

were supposed to open a business together. For my part in the business, I got an investment loan from Emma and equipment from my parents. The most valuable thing my mother could have given me was her collection of recipes. I was not a baker, but I could reasonably follow instructions or find people who could. Logan wanted to add a take-out restaurant, which I didn't object to as long as he managed that part of the business as I was even less adept at cooking than I was at baking. Logan was to handle the financial aspect of the business because he had had years of training working with his parents, and he also had a Master's in Accounting.

Logan acquired a space on his parents' plaza, and we started painting, fixing the bathrooms, putting in shelving and building showcases. About a month into the project, I was home fixing dinner one evening when Logan came to me and said, quite matter-of-factly, "We can't open the business. Dad decided to rent the place to someone else."

My mouth dropped. I cried, "But he can't do that! We've already started work and spent quite a bit of money. Is he giving us another space?"

"No," Logan said shaking his head, his expression glum. "I don't know what to tell you. He was offered far more than we can afford for the rent, and he's not passing it up."

"You need to talk to him. This is so unfair," I cried desperately, envisioning our hard work and our dreams going down the toilet.

Logan shrugged, "Sorry. There's nothing I can do about it. The building belongs to him. He can do whatever he wants. He already tore down the shelving and pulled up the showcases. All of it is gone."

"Gone where?" I asked, the walls of the large kitchen closing in on me. "We should at least get the material back to use somewhere else."

Logan looked uncomfortable as he shifted his weight from one leg to the other. "Sorry, we can't. Dad got rid of everything."

"What am I going to tell my sister? She needs to get her money back. Even if we're going to lose the rest of the money, at least get

95

her money back from your dad," I pleaded.

"Sorry, I can't do that. All the money that was spent is gone. It's money that can never be recovered. In business, that's what is called sunk cost," Logan said, his tone condescending.

I really wasn't interested in the business lesson. I just wanted it all to be a joke. Moreover, I wanted Logan to be as incensed as I was. He kept using the word sorry, but his expression said that he was anything but.

"How are we going to pay her back?" I cried, perturbed.

"We?" Logan smirked. "I didn't borrow any money from her."

My food was suddenly at odds with my stomach, but my dinner wasn't all I was at risk of losing. My head suddenly became buoyant, and my chest felt like an elephant had stubbornly decided that that was the perfect place to park its tush. My breathing, not faring any better, was sporadic.

"Oh . . . my . . . God. Are you kidding me? So . . . so, it's no longer "we" because I was the one who did the actual asking? What planet are you from? It doesn't work that way. You were the reason I asked for the loan in the first place, and you were supposed to draw up the contract. I don't know the first thing about APRs and crap." I fought back the tears of frustration welling behind my eyes, but I'd die before I gave Logan the satisfaction of seeing me shed one tear.

"Listen—" He stressed the word and glared at me hard as though his patience was being tested by a petulant child. "You deal with your sister, and I'll deal with my father."

I recognized when I was being handed the undesirable end of *the stick*, but I had to ask anyway. "So, you'll at least broach the subject with your father? It doesn't hurt to ask. Maybe he'll surprise you and be totally amenable."

Logan shook his head and sighed. "That sounds like it makes sense to you? Why do you do that? You're always saying stuff that makes no sense." He left the kitchen without a backward glance.

I felt sick, and far from grounded. My body was a mass of highly charged live wires—my nerves—all one hundred billion of them— frayed. I had to calm down. My skin was overheating. "God, put me out of my misery." Spontaneous combustion seemed an appealing alternative to calling my sister. Then, like rain, ice-cold sweat doused my body from head to toe . . . Maybe God has a sense of humor.

* * *

I was mad at Logan for months, and that anger extended to Constance and Eustace. I got over Eustace's part in the debacle in record time because I did not expect better of him. Based on what I had heard of his unscrupulous dealings with people, and through some experiences of my own, I had come to believe him capable of almost anything. I had, however, held out hope for Constance because she had expressed a few times that she wished we could cultivate a friendship. It, therefore, wasn't unreasonable for me to expect a gesture that facilitated that. Encouraging her husband to give us another space or give us our money back would have gone a far way towards mending the bridge. I didn't like a bone in Constance's body, but thanks to Abigail, I had come to realize that I didn't have to like her to forgive her.

So, I called my mother-in-law, which to date has been the most nerve-racking call I have ever made. I was literally sick to my stomach and covered in cold sweat. We exchanged pleasantries, quite awkwardly.

I hemmed and hawed a little, "Listen, Constance . . . the reason . . . the reason I'm calling is . . . we have some issues we need to resolve. Over the years, we haven't really gotten along, but it's not because I haven't wanted to. Frankly, it's been quite difficult. You like to be in control. You want to tell me what to wear, how to comb my hair, how to raise my children, how to relate to my husband, and when that doesn't work, you recruit people in your stead. You don't need to call my helper to find out if your son ate or call me to find out if I ironed his clothes. That kind of stuff might work for your sons, but . . . it doesn't work for me. You've also said and done some pretty hurtful things that I've found extremely hard to forgive, but I can't continue living like this."

I paused. It wasn't like her to allow me to go uninterrupted for so long. "Hello?" I said. Had we been cut off?

"I'm here," she said, her voice strained. And, as if I needed her permission, she coaxed, "Go on."

I really didn't want to get into the details. I wanted to do what I had called to do and get off the phone. "I'm not going to rehash any of it because it's really not necessary. It really isn't important whether or not you have any idea what I'm talking about. What is important is that I need to let you know that I forgive all of it."

I waited. Constance was silent for a while, and then she said quite flippantly, "I hear you."

Not deterred, I continued, my heart thumping viciously, "I know nobody is perfect, so in that vein, I would like to apologize if I've said or done anything to offend you."

"Okay," Constance said, obviously pleased and more receptive. I knew my apology had facilitated the turn-around. "I'm glad you called because it really is a prayer of mine that we get along. I don't want any bad blood between us. I haven't seen the children in a while. Everybody fine?"

"Yes, everybody is fine," I said, relieved she had changed the subject. "Thanks for being open to hearing what I had to say."

"No problem, man. We'll talk another time. Take care, and God bless."

When I hung up, I was happy. I had gotten the job done, chucking one of my heaviest burden-filled boxes. And I felt lighter.

* * *

One of my students, a six-year-old boy, started to misbehave during his tutoring session one day. He was acting wild and saying that he wanted to kill himself. When I tried to find out what was wrong, he stopped suddenly and looked me dead in the eyes, his eyes wild and devoid of even an iota of recognizable warmth. It was like staring into a black hole. We held each other's gaze, our eyes locked in a game of chicken. I was rattled, but I refused to let on. He was so little and yet looked so fierce. After a few tense moments, his blank expression changed.

He sneered and slanted his head a little to the left as he said, "Mi a demon." (I'm a demon.)

I know several expressions played on fast-forward across my face, the least severe of which was disbelief. "What did you say?" I asked, somehow hoping I had heard him wrong—but seeing the truth of it in his eyes.

He grinned widely. "Mi a demon," he repeated, his smile not reaching his eyes.

My skin crawled, but I continued to hold his gaze.

After a few moments, he smirked, slowly shook his head and tsked a few times. Then, he raised his chin defiantly, and looked at me sideways. "Mi wi kill yuh, yuh nuh. Mi wi kill yuh." (I will kill you, you know. I will kill you.)

"Tyrell," I said softly. I felt like I was being sucked into an abyss. I needed him to come out.

"Tyrell," I barely whispered. He was so still. "*Oh God*," I thought. "*Let him come back.*" I didn't want any of the other parents to come and see him like that. I could never explain it.

He just continued staring at me hard.

"Tyrell," I said a little firmer and held my breath.

"*Oh Lord, what am I going to tell this boy's father?*" I wondered. "*Maybe I'll just tell him that Tyrell wants to kill himself and leave out the part about the demon . . . but I can't not say anything. Oh my God, what am I going to do?"* I felt helpless. It's not like I could simply walk away as I had done before.

"I'll say he needs special prayer." Hopefully, somebody at his church would see what I was seeing.

As I watched on, Tyrell's eyes warmed, then slowly filled with tears. He ran and wrapped his skinny little arms around me tight. I stood stiffly with my hands trapped at my sides and murmured softly, "It's okay, Tyrell. I promise. You're going to be okay."

He missed a few sessions, but the next time I saw him, he grinned mischievously before running to hug me tight. "Hi, Auntie Jabez. Want one?" he asked, holding up a bag of sour worms.

* * *

One night, *I dreamed I saw two of my oldest and dearest friends from high school. I first ran into Rachel who wanted me to come hang out with her. Then, Kelly came along and invited me to a church program, pointing to a quaint, little church nesting atop a hill. Just then, Abigail walked towards us but stopped off in the distance. Although she hadn't spoken, I knew she was waiting for me.*

I turned to my two friends and said quite remorsefully, "Sorry guys. I have to go with Abigail." I walked away, leaving them behind.

What was that about? That dream was very strange. I had known Rachel and Kelly almost thirty years, and I knew Abigail—what?—two minutes?

What's more, when I told the dream to my mom, she said, "What you're telling me is very strange. By the way, who is this Abigail? Why would you walk away from your friends to go with her? You need to be careful. You're sure you're not in a cult?"

I rolled my eyes. "A cult? Seriously, Mother. Have you ever heard of a two-man cult?"

"Well, no—" I could almost hear the wheels turning as she racked her brain to come up with one.

I shook my head. "Mother, I don't understand the dream myself, but I unequivocally deny being in a cult. So, you can stop worrying."

"Okay Ma'am," my mom said. I could tell by her tone that she wasn't at all convinced.

* * *

Shortly after that dream, another followed. *I dreamed Abigail and I were trudging up an extraordinarily steep mountain. The hill appeared to go straight up—no slope. There were no ledges, ridges or crevices for handholds or on which to gain footing. There were no trees along the periphery to grab on to. Yet, inexplicably, the hill sloped just enough for us to climb, albeit with great difficulty. We plodded along, each step after unbelievably agonizing step.*

Sweat poured down my face, and I was sorely out of breath. "I can't go on."

"Come on," Abigail encouraged. "You've got to keep on going."

I took a few more steps, barely able to lift my feet off the ground then stopped again. Abigail, who was a few steps ahead of me, turned around.

She waved her hand. "Come on. Keep moving."

I rested my palms on my knees. "I want to turn back," I huffed.

"You can't go back," she said patiently.

I looked at the straight drop behind me and I saw the truth of it. There was no turning back. Not only was it impossible to make the descent, there was nothing but ruins left behind. I stopped every step I took, and Abigail kept encouraging me to keep moving—all the while inching further and further ahead of me. I became so preoccupied with my distress, at one point, that I didn't notice that I was all alone until I heard her call my name. I looked around but didn't see her.

"Up here," she called out. I looked up and there she was lying on her stomach, peering down at me. "There's a ledge. You just need to pull yourself up."

I groaned. She sounded way too cheery. I was so exhausted, I could barely stand. There was no way my arms could possibly bear the weight of my entire body.

"Come on," Abigail coaxed.

I remained rooted.

"The ground is level. All you have to do is pull yourself up."

I slowly moved closer and stretched my arms up. They didn't reach. I moaned.

"Come on. Jump up and grab on."

I jumped, trying desperately to grab hold but had no success. Tears poured down my face. I jumped again and missed. This went on for what seemed like forever until I finally grabbed hold of the ledge and laboriously pulled myself up. Besides encouraging me, Abigail made no move to assist me. Once I was able to stand up, my eyes swept the breath-taking panorama, and I marveled at the vastness laid out before us. We were standing on the pinnacle of a gargantuan rock. And the ground was solid.

I couldn't wait to tell Abigail about my dream the next morning. I called her as soon as I woke up. "Last night I had the strangest dream. I dreamed we were walking up a mountain, but the mountain was like none I've ever seen. It didn't slope. It appeared to go straight up."

She gasped. "Stop!"

"What?" I asked.

"I have to tell you my dream first," she said excitedly. I could envision her flapping her hands fast. "A couple nights ago, I dreamed I was going up a steep mountain on a motorbike with someone hanging on for dear life on the back. I couldn't see who it was because we were both wearing helmets. However, I wondered who would be crazy to trust me enough to go on such a treacherous ride. The only person I could think of was my mother. My passenger asked, "Do you think we can make it?" I looked back at what was behind us and said, "We have to because we can't turn back." We rode for only a short while before the bike flipped, landing at the bottom of the mountain. It smashed into pieces, but my passenger and I were not hurt."

I shrieked. "What? Describe this mountain."

"The mountain appeared to go straight up—no slope. I've never seen a mountain like this. The surface was smooth and had no rocks or gravel."

My heart raced. "You have to hear my dream."

I proceeded to tell her my dream ending with, "My dream is a continuation of yours. It picks up where your dream leaves off. That crazy passenger was me."

"Oh my God. I can't believe this!"

"Neither can I," I said, my mind racing—the words all but tumbling from my lips, "How can two people have a dream about the same thing? And, what's more, one dream being a continuation of the other. Now I understand what the dream with Rachel and Kelly meant. I could not go with them because you were waiting for me to start our climb."

"This is unbelievable," Abigail fought to speak slowly. "I didn't tell you about the dream because I thought it silly. Two people going up a hill on a bike? What's that? I couldn't imagine that that meant anything."

"I know, right? This is huge."

We talked about the dreams for a couple hours that day and almost every day for months after that. While we were amazed by the awesomeness of it all, we didn't know what it meant. We felt trepidation because such a journey could only signify hardship, but we were encouraged because the completion of the journey was hope exemplified.

* * *

One night, a few weeks after the dream, Logan and I were in the kitchen when he said out of the blue, "The guys are almost done with the work at the shop."

I knitted my brow. "What?"

"The workmen are almost done with the work," he said.

I was confused. "What work?"

Logan looked at me as though I were dense. "The work at the hardware store. I want to open in the next two weeks."

Was I supposed to know what he was talking about? "What hardware store? We're opening a hardware store?" I asked, bewildered. Why was I just hearing about this? I was used to Logan keeping me in the dark, but this was ridiculous.

"We?" Logan asked mockingly. "We—" He swung his index finger back and forth between us. "—are not doing a thing. If you want to open a business, go open one for yourself."

I felt as though I had been punched in the stomach, but I was not going to give Logan the satisfaction of seeing that hurt. "Fine," I said nonchalantly. "Do your thing. Have you picked out a name?"

"Yeah," he said, sticking his chest out ever so slightly I might have missed it had I not known him so well. "It's Constance and Son Co. Ltd."

There was a bit of a delayed reaction, and then I started hooting with laughter. I struggled to catch my breath. "Wha'?" I asked and burst out laughing again. It took a while, but I stopped laughing long enough to ask, "You're kidding, right? Are you pulling my legs?"

"Yeah, man. Laugh," he said, angrily. "You never support me in anything I do."

I not only reeled from the hostility in his voice but the falsehood of his accusation. "I never support you, Logan? Really? You know what? If telling yourself and everybody else that makes you feel better

104

about what you've done, then fine. I was there when you went back to school for a second bachelor's degree, a master's degree and several certifications. Do you realize that by the time Nathan was ten years old we had moved ten times? I followed you everywhere. If that's not being supportive, then I don't know what is," I said, close to tears.

I spun around to leave but pulled up short and scoffed, "Oh, and by the way, don't think that I'm not aware of your treachery. It's obvious you and your parents came to some agreement about the restaurant. Yet, you made it seem as though it was all on your father because you knew I'd never confront him. I heard Eustace tell you that no son of his was going to run a soup kitchen. Guess he convinced you. But for you to conspire to cut me out? That's unconscionable."

Logan raised both hands in the air and yelled, "Now hold up. Don't talk about my parents. This has nothing to do with them."

My eyebrows shot up. "Really? Where did you get the money?"

He clenched his jaw and said defensively, "The bank."

I chuckled, not caring that Logan might be offended. I was past sparing his feelings because it couldn't be more obvious that he cared naught about mine. "What bank? The Bank of Eustace and Constance?"

Logan glared at me and said, "Yeah . . . laugh. I'm going to make this business a huge success, and I don't need you to do it. As a matter of fact, I don't want you anywhere near it."

I shrugged. "Fine, Constance's son. Good luck." I jeered, giving Logan not one, but two middle fingers, as I walked backwards towards the staircase. I barely made it upstairs before I burst into tears.

About an hour later, a WhatsApp message came in from someone I hadn't spoken to in years, and who had just a week before made contact to say she would love to hear from me.

The message read:

> "My dear brothers and sisters, take note of this: Everyone should be quick to listen, slow to speak and slow to become angry" (James 1:19, NIV).

I almost felt ashamed of myself . . . almost.

* * *

In the weeks that followed, I couldn't remotely get past what Logan had done so as to begin reconciling what I had done. The Bible speaks of a time to hate (Ephesians 3:8, NIV), and the circumstances warranted that. I wallowed in that hate, and it grew exponentially. And then, God stepped in.

I dreamed that two angels led Abigail and me to the edge of a body of water. Just as we got there, we heard rumbling in the distance. Huge chunks of rock and snow broke away from their bed and came tumbling down the side of the mountain—almost immediately losing definition and morphing into a huge mass. As the mass careened down the hill, it gathered more snow. Both angels stepped into the water, and sweeping their hands outward, motioned for us to get in. Abigail got in without hesitating.

I, on the other hand, stood stiffly on the shore. "You've got to be kidding! I'm not getting in. I'm afraid of the water. Besides, I can't swim," I said indignantly.

The angel on my right calmly said, "You need to get in and go under. That's the only way you'll be saved."

I shook my head and stood my ground. Abigail said nothing and neither did the other angel.

A little more sternly, the angel said, "You need to get in."

"I can't," I whined. "I'm afraid. There must be another way."

"There is no other way."

I glanced around nervously as the rumbling got louder and the mass rolled closer. I had no choice. Reluctantly, I got in, and we all went under. I prepared to panic as water covered my head and filled my nose and ears. However, the panic never came because I was actually breathing fine. We descended to the ocean bed and entered a cave. No sooner had we gotten inside, we heard a loud rumble and felt the earth violently quake.

Of the two of us, I was the one quick to fight and prone to panic. The dream spoke to the trials and tribulations of life. It was God's assurance that no matter the circumstance, He would see me through. He needed me to know that while His way might not be the easiest, it is the only way. However, it requires an inordinate amount of trust as well as total surrender. That dream went a long way in restoring my soul. I let go of what I couldn't control—and even ended up rooting for Logan's business . . . albeit from afar off.

* * *

Despite the mountain and avalanche dreams which were assuring and reassuring, Abigail and I could not help but feel overwhelmed at times. God, however, is so patient and kind that He constantly reminds me how much He cares for me. Once, when I felt like giving up, I pleaded with God for a respite, and He took me to the edge of a cliff.

I dreamed that I was so downtrodden that I decided to take my own life. I went to the edge of a high cliff overlooking a beach, closed my eyes and jumped. I landed safely on my feet. I felt no pain—only the sand beneath my feet and the breeze against my skin. I gasped and opened my eyes. I looked around in disbelief, taking in the beach I had only moments before been afraid to even look at, it was so far down. When I looked at the spot from which I had jumped, there no longer was a cliff there, but a ledge jutting from a rock. Jumping from the cliff had been tantamount to jumping from a chair. Astounded, I examined my clothing and touched various parts of my body, checking for broken bones. I also looked for scratches. Nothing. I was unscathed. My heart sank. I had failed to kill myself. I couldn't even do that right. I spotted a cave in the distance and thought it might be a good place to hide away forever. When I entered the cave, however, Abigail was there. She was kneeling on the ground stacking money in piles. By the time she reached the third pile, the first and second piles disappeared. She would then have to start over. However, the outcome was the same every time.

Abigail's part of the dream spoke to the financial challenges she was facing. However, it also confirmed a promise God had made to increase her store of seeds so that she could, through generosity, bless others (2 Corinthians 9: 10-11, NIV). My jumping from the cliff unharmed confirmed God's promise in Psalm 91 to protect me, to rescue me, to be with me in times of trouble and to instruct His angels concerning me so that I come to no harm—not even by my own hands. What's more, Abigail's journey and mine seem to be inextricably intertwined—whereby I speak into her life and she, in turn, speaks into mine.

* * *

Over a period of time, Abigail's family and mine spent more and more time together. Sometimes we would meet up in Florida to shop. I was standing with Abigail's husband George one day in a business establishment. Abigail had just left to use the restroom when a man came over to us. He and George greeted each other heartily. Then, the man noticed me and asked George, "Who is this?"

Without the slightest hesitation, George said, "This is my wife's sister." I had to quickly mask my surprise before either man noticed.

The man proffered a hand and warmly said, "Nice to meet you." I grinned widely as his fingers closed around mine.

A Message from the Tree

I dreamed I was seated in a crowded room filled with chatter so low and incessant it sounded like bees humming. Someone addressed me. I looked around, but everyone was engaged in conversation. I heard the voice again but could not discern the source nor what was being said. Then, I heard the voice say, "Go outside."

I got up and immediately walked outside onto a large lawn with people clustered in small groups. I was immediately drawn to an imposing tree that stood alone in the middle of the property—with a trunk of tremendous circumference and large, high branches. I figured it would offer the best shade against the sweltering sun. I leaned against the trunk and watched as people laughed, played games and enjoyed picnics.

I heard a loud rumbling sound as the tree behind me shook against my back. I looked down and saw the earth burst open as roots became visible. I should have run, but I couldn't. I backed away from the tree, watching transfixed as it shook. The earth continued to burst open, forming large crevices as huge roots surfaced. What was even more shocking was that I glanced up to see that the tree had a face.

"What are you doing?" I shouted over the noise.

"I'm going to go throw myself across a river to save a community of people."

"But if you do, you're going to die!"

"I have to," the tree calmly replied.

"Why?"

"Because it's what I've been commanded to do."

"What?" I cried in disbelief.

"One day you'll be able to tell the rocks to move, the mountains to move and the trees to move. But you're not ready."

And with that, the tree tramped away from me in the direction of the river.

The dream upset me somewhat. I had tried my entire life to be a good Christian—to be kind, helpful and caring. Why would I not be ready? What would it take for me to be ready? I believed I could do anything if only God gave me the power.

* * *

A couple weeks later, *Nathan dreamed that he and I were at a train station. As we got to the crowded platform, we saw a girl with eyes an odd shade of blue. Her pupils, instead of being round, were long vertical black slits—like those of a snake. Upon seeing us, she started towards us. But I held out my hand, and she stopped dead in her tracks.*

Her eyes turned normal instantly. "I'm sorry," she said before turning and walking away.

"Did you see the chains?" I asked.

"What chains?" Nathan craned his neck to catch a glimpse of her, but she was gone.

"She was bound by chains, but I'm not the one to free her," I said regretfully.

Nathan's dream gave me pause. I had no idea what it meant, but I knew better than to dismiss it because, eerily, a few of Nathan's dreams had turned out to be accurately predictive. I wondered about the girl. Who was she? Why had she started towards us? Did she know us? Maybe her intention was to ask for help. Did I do the right thing in turning her away? Maybe I should have tried to free her. After a couple days, I decided to simply wait on God instead of worry about the meaning of the dream because, whatever the meaning, it would be revealed in due time.

* * *

A few months later, *I dreamed that I was atop a tower with The Master. There was a war raging, and I was a part of an army. The Master gave directives to his soldiers, who each possessed phenomenal skills—as this was no ordinary war. He sent troops out strategically, and when their jobs were done, they returned and others were deployed.*

When it was my turn to go, I cowered in a corner. "I'm not ready. Please send someone else," I cried as The Master towered over me, his imposing figure eclipsing the light.

His voice thundered and rolled. "No."

Shaking uncontrollably, I peered up at him. "But I'm not ready." I was close to tears.

"It is too late," he said calmly but firmly.

My heart sank. Up until the point I was sent into battle, I believed that I was ready because I was armed with tremendous skills and power. I looked away, unable to bear the severe disapproval on The Master's face.

This dream bothered me because it highlighted that I was controlled by fear. I couldn't be mad about the dream because it was true. The Bible states, "For everyone to whom much is given, from him much will be required (Luke 12:48, NKJV), and I had been given much. Some of my actions, and adversely my inaction, had been partly due to fear: fear of ridicule, fear of ostracism, fear of erring, fear of failure. All of these fears should have been tempered by the fear of falling out of favor with God, but they were not always.

111

* * *

Almost a year later, Christine *dreamed that the devil came into our house. He went from room to room, leaving what appeared to be apples behind. She shouted for me. As soon as he became aware that he had been seen, he fled the house.*

The dream worried me, but I tried not to show it. I also tried to convince Christine that she had nothing to worry about. We didn't discuss it again.

A few months after that, my kids and I were discussing some spiritual matters. Christine, however, seemed a bit discombobulated. At some point, she fell to her knees and cried out. It was a cry like I'd never heard. Chills went down my spine.

Unnerved, Nathan said to me, "Is Chrissy alright?"

Michael looked concerned but remained quiet.

"Yes, she is," I said, trying to sound calm, however feeling anything but.

Frowning, he asked, "Are you sure, Mom?"

"Yes," I said firmly, glancing over at Christine.

She was still kneeling. She appeared to be in pain as she slowly rocked back and forth. I cautiously approached her and placed my hand on her back. She jumped. "Let's go eat," I said and gently helped her up.

I quickly gave the boys dinner and sent them to the den to eat so that I could be alone with Christine in the kitchen. I shared her dinner— all the while stealing glances at her—not wanting to believe what I was seeing. She had only one forkful of food and then set her fork aside. I could not ignore the truth any longer.

I approached her and said softly, "Christine."

She didn't answer. Instead, she slowly raised her head.

A beast focused its eyes on me. I went cold.

"Oh my God," I thought. *"This can't be happening. Not to my*

child."

Although terror rose up and closed its fist around my throat, I managed to call, "Christine."

No answer.

I held the gaze of the beast and called more firmly, "Chrissy."

Christine looked at me and weakly said, "Yes, Mom."

"Are you alright?"

Her eyes pleading, desperate and sad, she weakly whispered, "No." I'm not sure I would have heard her had I not been looking at her.

"Okay," I said softly.

Then she was gone.

As Beast stared at me, I thought, *"Oh my God. This can't be for real!"*

I grabbed Christine's hand and all but dragged her behind me. I told the boys to stay inside no matter what. When we got outside, I faced Christine. As my eyes met the beast's, the pit feeling in my stomach intensified.

I placed my right hand on her forehead and said to the beast, "I see you. You've been here long enough, but you have to leave tonight."

Nothing could have prepared me for what transpired next. Christine immediately fell to her knees, her torso slumping forward. She banged her head extremely hard on the concrete driveway. Then, she vomited up a substance that was as black as tar. Frightened, I jumped back. However, I quickly regained my composure. I couldn't afford to show fear. As I re-approached Christine, the most horrific roar came from her mouth as Beast let its displeasure be known. Christine was bleeding from a gash on her forehead, so I lay my hand atop her head instead.

In the most authoritative voice I could muster, I said, "Come out, I command you in the name of Jesus Christ of Nazareth!"

Beast's only response was to roar even louder.

Maybe I hadn't said it with enough authority, so I said with more force, "Come out, I command you in the name of Jesus Christ of

Nazareth!"

Christine twisted and writhed as Beast roared even louder. The roaring was non-stop, with pauses only long enough for Christine to draw breath.

My husband, who was inside, opened the door and asked, "What are you doing to her? The neighbors are calling about the noise. You need to get her inside."

I was furious at the interference. I tried to stall. I couldn't take her back inside the house. "It's okay. I need to talk to her."

"Well, do it in inside."

When I didn't move, he frowned and said firmly, "Listen, talk to her inside. She can't be out here making all this noise. The neighbors are concerned."

Reluctantly, I led Christine into the house. When we got to the dining room, Logan held her shoulders firmly. He stared her straight in the eyes and said, "Listen, you can't be carrying on like this! What's wrong with you?"

Beast roared as Christine twisted, trying to get away.

"Sit down," Logan said, pulling out a chair for her.

Beast ramped up the roaring and demonstrated its anger, as Christine started pushing the dining table and pitching over chairs.

Scowling, Logan asked, "What did you do to her?"

"I didn't do anything to her!" I scowled back at him, indignant.

I couldn't bring myself to tell him the truth. I didn't know how he would respond, given his negative reaction to all things spiritual that came from my lips.

"Well, what's wrong with her?"

I didn't respond.

He held Christine's shoulder. "Chrissy."

She didn't respond.

Frustrated, he said, "I'm taking her to the hospital."

My heart raced, but still, I said nothing.

As we drove away from our house, I mustered up some courage.

"Listen . . . we can't take her to the hospital."

"Why?"

My heart thumped loudly, and I stuttered. "No . . . No . . . no doctor can help her." I paused for a split moment, took a deep breath and quickly added, "But I know someone who can."

"Who?" Logan asked, his voice laced with skepticism. "It's clear she needs a hospital, and the sooner we get her there the better. You know how long the wait time can be in these hospitals."

Why did Logan always behave like I was incompetent? He was hardly ever home and the kids had more than merely survived—they had thrived. "Just drive. I'll tell you where to go." I was really annoyed at this point. "You need to trust me when I tell you that she doesn't need a hospital. They're just going to put her on the psych ward and dope her up. Going to the hospital would be a mistake."

I pointed and said, "Turn right here."

"Jabez, you better know what you're doing," Logan warned, as he made the turn. I let out a huge sigh of relief.

Although the ride was only about two miles, it stretched out forever as Beast roared incessantly. When we arrived at Mrs. Foster's—the woman who was to pray for Christine—Logan stayed in the car, and I went to talk to her. She couldn't help me because she had just given birth.

Disappointed, I returned to the van. It was time to come clean to Logan. "Listen. Christine needs prayer and Mrs. Foster can't do it. Do you know anybody who knows anything about demon possession?"

Logan's eyes widened. "What? How did this happen? Was she playing Charlie Charlie at school?" he asked, referring to a game played by some teenagers in the movie *Ouija 3*. Students in some of the schools on the island, including the one my kids attended, took to playing the game. For weeks, there were reports of strange happenings, like mass faintings, peculiar behavior and unexplained thumps and thuds in walls. Charlie? Really? So . . . sensational stories of a demon named Charlie were more believable than anything I had told Logan?

How could he believe in secular supernatural beings of urban legends and folklore, but not believe in Biblical supernatural beings?

I shook my head. "No. This isn't Charlie." I hoped he wouldn't ask me how I knew that. Do you know anybody who deals with this kind of thing?"

"Yes. Pastor Bowman," he said, immediately dialing the pastor's number. Another shocker. How did he happen to have the number of a pastor who dealt with demons?

The pastor told Logan to put the phone to Christine's ear. Whatever he said infuriated the beast. It roared even louder and caused Christine to start thrashing about. Her arms and legs flailed, and she banged her head on the door. Frightened, I tried to restrain her.

"How do you know Pastor Bowman," I yelled over my shoulder. I was on my knees, hanging over the back of the front seat, struggling to hold Christine still. We couldn't afford to take her to a flake. This pastor had to be authentic.

"I met him at a convention I was playing at and saw him at work. He cast demons out of several people that night. We got to talking afterward, and he gave me his number."

That would explain Logan referring to himself as "Keysie" when he identified himself to the pastor. In Jamaica, nicknames are a thing, and a nickname sticks all the more if the person being tagged really hates it. People get nicknames based on what they do, where they come from, how they look, things they commonly say, etc. My husband played keyboard in a band, hence the name.

I eventually had to give up restraining Christine—who seemed to have the strength of a dozen men—or risk getting hurt. Logan and I didn't speak to each other the rest of the way. The road was eerily lonely, and we seemed to be getting sucked in by the darkness of the night. Given the circumstances, the moon was befittingly stingy with its light. My blood curdled every time Beast roared, and I struggled to quash the sense of hopelessness threatening to choke me.

We picked Pastor Bowman up from his house on the way to his

church. He and my husband exchanged pleasantries and started talking. I butted in when Pastor Bowman mentioned the possibility that Beast might be Charlie. "This isn't Charlie."

Pastor Bowman looked a little taken aback by my tone. Frankly, if he couldn't even tell what he was dealing with, maybe he wasn't the man for the job. I decided to help him out. "And, by the way, Christine had a dream a few months prior."

Pastor Bowman held up a hand and said, "No. Don't tell me anything until after I'm done."

I wanted to argue that the dream was important but held my tongue. I had to trust that there was a reason Mrs. Foster was unavailable because God is intentional in what He does.

By the time we finally got to the church, Beast had gone quiet. Pastor Bowman and two other men approached Christine while a young woman, Logan and I stood on the sidelines.

In a firm voice, Pastor Bowman asked the beast, "Who sent you?"

No response.

"What is your name?"

No response.

He turned to me with amazement and a bit of amusement on his face and said, "This girl's spirit is so strong. She has it so this demon can't hear or speak."

My heart skipped a beat. That would explain why Beast had suddenly gone quiet. Good for Christine! She was actually fighting back.

He then turned back to the beast, touched Christine's ear and said, "Speak!"

Beast railed up and roared. The two men held Christine.

Pastor Bowman began again. "What's your name?"

Again, Beast railed up and roared, throwing its head back—its claws curling.

"Who sent you?"

Beast thrashed about and roared even louder, refusing to speak.

Pastor Bowman asked the demon several more times who had sent it, but its only response was a roar.

"What were you sent to do?" Pastor Bowman continued, not deterred by Beast's lack of cooperation.

Beast railed and roared some more.

Pastor Bowman looked over to the woman beside me and said to her, "What do you see?"

"A beast and a snake. The beast is in charge," she said.

I gasped and said, "You can see?"

She nodded.

"But I only saw the beast," I said breathlessly.

"There's a snake as well," she said softly.

A snake?

The girl that was bound in Nathan's dream!

I shivered, and my teeth chattered. I had not done anything to help her then, and I was helpless to do so now.

Beast's roar once again caught my attention. Pastor Bowman touched Christine's hand with some water he had in a bottle. That seemed to cause the beast tremendous pain. It roared loudly—its claws curling. Christine's body contorted, and her arms flailed about. The men were having a hard time holding her. Pastor Bowman enlisted my husband's help, and I watched in horror as the three men struggled to maintain hold of Christine's small one-hundred-pound frame.

Pastor Bowman touched Christine's hand again and said, "Release her hands. Now!" Christine's fingers uncurled, but then the fingers of her other hand formed claws. Pastor Bowman used the water on that hand, and then the fingers on the first hand curled again. Each time Pastor Bowman touched one of Christine's hands, he would give the beast an order. And, each time, Beast roared and fought against the hands holding Christine.

Pastor Bowman moved to Christine's feet, and the same thing happened as with her hands. Her feet kept curling into hooves. Pastor Bowman then moved to Christine's stomach and each time he touched her stomach, she threw up a little of the same black-tar-looking substance she had left on our driveway. He gave her some of the water to drink, and she threw up some more.

Then, Beast threw Christine's body so far backwards, she was almost lying horizontal. It curled its claws and hooked its hooves together. I gasped. It looked like Beast was attempting to hold on to Christine's body on the inside—the way one would hold on to the hood of a car to keep from being thrown . . . or, maybe the way someone would curl his toes in a pair of flipflops to keep them on his feet. I was mortified. I felt faint. No matter what command Pastor Bowman gave, Beast would not let go.

With the passing of time, I started to worry that Pastor Bowman would fail, and Christine would be lost to us forever. I had to push that thought from my mind with prayer. It was as I started to pray that I realized that I had been so enthralled by what was happening that I had failed to reach out to God the entire time. After I prayed, a sense of calm blanketed me. I watched, no longer anxious, and no matter how Christine's body thrashed about, I remained thus. After a long while, Christine's head finally lolled, and she went still. My heart galloped. Was it over? I held my breath as Pastor Bowman called on a legion of angels to dispatch the demons. After more than two hours, Christine was finally free.

Everybody sat quietly, physically and mentally drained. Christine could hardly keep her torso up. She leaned heavily on me, and I wrapped my arms tightly around her. I couldn't stand the silence. "How could this have happened?" I asked Pastor Bowman.

"Sometimes people use demons to do their bidding, but these demons were sent by the devil himself. Demons usually say their names, who sent them and what they were sent to do. But not in this case. This case was really tough. I had to call a legion of angels because the demons were a legion," he said.

My stomach pitted. *Oh my God! A legion?* I thought. I wanted to throw up. I listened to Pastor Bowman and Logan talk for a while—

too afraid to speak I was shaking so badly. After about fifteen minutes, I calmed enough to tell Pastor Bowman the details of Christine's dream. Pastor Bowman listened intently and then said, "God is granting Christine authority to dispatch demons and that power will be in her right hand." He turned to Christine and asked, "Are you willing to accept it?"

Too exhausted to speak, she nodded weakly. Pastor Bowman then laid hands on her and blessed her.

* * *

The only reason I jumped into action with Christine was that she was my child. It was not faith I possessed that night, however, but hope. Like the disciples in Matthew 17:14-21, who lacked the faith they needed to cast a demon out of a boy, I lacked the faith it took to be able to say to the beast, "Come out," and have it comply. Consequently, authority and power are useless in the absence of faith—tantamount to arming oneself with an unloaded weapon.

The tree had been right. I was not ready.

Baptism by Fire

A round the time I had the dream about the tree, several members of the church congregation, including Pastor, approached my kids about baptism. The kids reluctantly went with Logan to a few classes. There, they were schooled on the relevance of baptism in the Christian faith and the importance of taking that step. Family members stepped in to coax them as well. Constance was unrelenting, even driving them to the classes herself when Logan was unavailable. However, the kids were resistant. When I asked them why, they all said that while they understood the significance of baptism, they weren't ready. I told them that it was alright and that they should never make any decision regarding their faith to please anyone.

* * *

Roughly one year later, Christine was struggling with issues stemming from her run-in with the demons that had plagued her. She was fearful and anxious, and she refused to sleep alone. Night after night, I prayed with her extensively and reassured her that "God has not given us a spirit of fear; but of power, and of love, and of a sound mind" (2 Timothy 1:7, NKJV). I was strong and reassuring when I spoke to her, but my heart splintered into a million pieces when I was alone.

One night I desperately reasoned with God, "I refuse to believe that You kept her for however long she had to fight, only to have her fall apart now that the threat is over. Then, what would have been the point? It would mean that You failed, and we both know You cannot fail. She has to be okay!" As I said that, a calm enveloped me, and I knew Christine would be whole again.

Christine shook me awake one night. "Mom," she said shakily, "I had a weird dream."

My heart sank, "It's okay. Just pray and go back to sleep."

I reached over and gently stroked the side of her face.

"But I can't," she insisted.

"Chrissy, you're going to be okay. Just go back to sleep. We'll talk about the dream in the morning."

"Mom," she wailed, "my hand burns."

I sat up. "What?"

She held her hand up, but I couldn't see so I got up and turned on the lights.

"Let me see," I said, taking her hand.

My mouth fell open.

"What happened to your hand?" I shouted, aghast at the sight of her blisteringly red palm. "How did you burn it?"

"It happened when I was sleeping," she said, just staring down at her red palm, offering no further explanation.

"What happened?" I coaxed, anxious and impatient.

"I saw a man and woman quarreling," Christine said with a faraway look in her eyes as though she were back in her dream. "As I watched them, a boy came and stood beside me. I didn't pay him any mind because I was so focused on the man and woman. They argued for a while and then they walked down the road, so I followed them. I didn't realize until I got inside a supermarket that the boy had followed me all that way. I stood in the aisle watching him, wondering what he was up to, and then he started coming towards me. Sensing something wasn't right about him, I stretched out my right hand. He became paralyzed all of a sudden. Then, cymbals clashed, and a light flashed.

He changed into a beast with weird eyes and a symbol on his forehead. I said, "Demon, I rebuke you in the name of the Lord!" As soon as I said that, I was transported to a white space without any windows or doors. Then, I heard a voice say, "Hold your head up." When I woke up, my hand was burning."

"What?" I said, both shocked and amazed. "That's good. You realized what it was and dealt with it. Do you know what this means? You don't have to be afraid anymore because God has really given you the power to vanquish demons."

Christine nodded and grinned widely as the enormity of it sank in, "Yeah."

I rubbed her palm with some burn cream and prayed with her. In the morning, the first thing I did when I woke up was check her palm. The redness was gone.

After that night, a spark was lit in Christine. She came to me less and less for reassurance. She no longer questioned whether her thoughts were her own. She no longer feared closing her eyes at night. And whenever I asked her if she was okay and she said yes, I could see that she believed it.

* * *

One day, a few months later, God said to me, "The children need to be baptized."

"Ok, God. By whom?" I asked.

"Pastor James," He replied.

"Okay, God. Where?"

"Out in the open water."

"Okay, God."

I immediately told the kids about the message, and I expected shock or maybe apprehension. Instead, I got huge face-splitting grins and tons of wows and reallys.

"When do we do this?" Nathan asked excitedly.

I shrugged. "I dunno. I didn't get a time."

"So, when are you going to call Pastor James?" he pressed.

"As soon as possible. But I wanted to talk to you guys first," I said, looking from one to the other.

When I was little, one promise I had made to myself was that my children, when I had them, would have what I never had—a voice. Each could raise that voice loud and clear, not hampered by the adage, "Children should be seen and not heard." And, in my case, sometimes neither seen nor heard. Having a voice is synonymous with having freedom, which affords choices. If the kids were too little to have a voice, then I vowed that I would be that voice. A little dramatic, true, but I did not like that my feelings didn't count and that if I didn't like something, I was expected to just suck it up. If I protested, there was no sparing the rod and spoiling this child.

Michael and Christine had yet to speak. "What are you thinking Michael?" I asked.

It was especially important for me to hear from him. He was quiet and could easily be overlooked. When Michael entered the third grade, his teacher stopped me one evening when I went to pick him up. She wanted to know if Michael could speak. When I expressed confusion at the question, she explained that since he had been in her class, he hadn't spoken a single word. I looked at her as though she had two heads and a horn. They were two months into the term!

"I'm thinking this is actually pretty cool," he replied, quite pensive.

"Me too," Christine chimed in.

"You know, Mom, I get it," Nathan said, speaking rapidly, unable to contain his excitement. "We couldn't have gotten baptized when everybody was trying to push us to. It wasn't the right time. We talked about it, but none of us could put a finger on what was holding us back. I don't know about Chrissy and Michael, but I don't feel like that anymore. I know that this is the right time. I can't explain how I know it, but I do."

Christine and Michael nodded simultaneously.

"This is really amazing," I said in awe. However, a small part of me wondered if they were simply agreeing because they wanted to please me. I so hoped that was not the case.

Nathan's face lit up. "Mom, Christine couldn't have been baptized before because what happened to her had to happen. And when it did, she couldn't be baptized like that. She had to be okay first. Because we have to do this together, Michael and I couldn't have been baptized either."

Michael was referring to Christine's possession. It sounded so simple now to hear him say it. "You're right, Nathan. Nothing happens before the time. This is all so incredible. I'll call Pastor James as soon as possible," I said, gathering them for a group hug.

* * *

Logan . . . I had to tell Logan. That, I wasn't looking forward to. However, I told him that night. Incredibly, he went on as if I hadn't spoken, "There's going to be a baptism at Hope Springs next month. It's going be a joint event with our sister church, so it will be a bigger than usual event. I'll contact Pastor and let him know that the kids are ready to be baptized. That way they'll be penciled in with the others."

"What?" I asked, annoyed. "Did you hear anything I said, Logan? The kids can't be baptized like that. It has to be how God says, where God says and who God says."

Logan ignored me and said, "The church hasn't had a baptism in quite a while, and Head Office has come down on Pastor about that. The problem was that the pool needed to be repaired. Then, when it was repaired, there was a problem with water because of the drought

. . . but the water issue has been resolved."

I rolled my eyes and sighed heavily. "Logan," I began with all the patience I could muster. "None of that matters. I'm going to talk to Pastor James about baptizing the kids."

"I want you to hear me, and hear me good," Logan spoke deliberately, his eyes piercing, his voice hard. "You can't just go off and do your own thing. The kids are mine too. If you do this, you and I are going to have big problems."

"Logan, *you're* not hearing *me*," I said, raising my voice. "I'm not doing my own thing. Far from it. I don't know about you, but if I disobey God, there are real-life consequences for me. I especially can't disobey Him about the kids." I could have segued into the dream of the three rings. However, what would have been the point? Logan had already firmly planted both feet, and I would only be spurring him to dig his heels in further.

I decided to lay the argument to rest because I was getting nowhere. "Can we talk about this another time?"

Logan shrugged. "Sure." His tone was noncommittal.

I sighed. "*I guess we're going to have problems*," I thought as I walked away.

A couple days later, I approached Logan. "Do you have Pastor James' number? He must have changed it. I'm getting a "no longer in service" recording," I said, crossing all my fingers.

Sometimes I would say something, and Logan would say I never said it. Or, he would swear he told me something he never did—a very typical, contentious issue. In this instance, he was distracted by one of his greatest loves—his cell phone. "What number do you have?"

I rattled the numbers off to him.

"That's the number I have as well. Maybe you can try Lowell," he suggested.

"Thanks," I said, exiting the kitchen. I shook my head as I climbed the stairs. Logan never spared me the slightest glance the entire conversation.

126

* * *

As soon as I got the number from Lowell, I called Pastor James. After warning him that what I was about to tell him was going to sound pretty crazy, I told him about my conversation with God. When I got to the part about the baptism having to be in the open water, Pastor James surprised me by saying he baptizes in a river, not inside a church. Without any qualms, he agreed to baptize the kids, stating that it was what God had commanded; therefore, he had to obey.

Pastor James and I spoke a few times leading up to the baptism. In one of our conversations, he explained that candidates for baptism normally got counseling through a series of classes. I informed him that the kids had already attended a few classes at church, and I was confident that they were ready. Pastor James seemed satisfied with that.

Each time I talked to Logan, he made an argument for baptism at Hope Springs. It didn't matter how many times I countered that obedience to God trumped tradition and legalism, he wouldn't budge. I eventually dropped the subject.

I struggled internally as I made the arrangements to make the two-hour trip to get the kids baptized. But, when the date was decided, I got a distinct message not to tell Logan what it was. I couldn't believe what I was hearing, "God, I know this is what you say that I'm to do, but this is going to cause bigger problems between Logan and me. He is never going to forgive me. What am I supposed to do?

"Is Logan bigger than God?" God asked.

It was so much more than a question. And it was all I needed. I put all worry about Logan's reaction to rest.

* * *

The night before the baptism, as soon as we got home and went upstairs, we heard Michael's puppy Milo cry out. The cries were shrill and coming in rapid succession. Michael ran through his bedroom and out onto his balcony.

"Mom, Milo fell off the balcony!" he shouted, not realizing we were right behind him. Milo's cage door was open.

"Can you see him?" I asked from my spot way over in a corner of the balcony. I was deathly afraid of heights. The balcony, although on the second floor of our house, was actually three stories up because the back of the property sloped.

"No. It's too dark," Christine shouted, her voice panicked.

Somebody needed to check on Milo, and it wasn't going to be me. My stomach and my head did strange things at the sight of blood and gore, and there was bound to be some, given the size of the Yorkie. I called outside to Logan who was closing the gate. He had taken several animal science courses in college for his agriculture degree, so he was not squeamish. When he came from the backyard holding Milo, the kids rushed outside to tend to the puppy.

"How does he look?" I called through a window.

Never having mastered the art of sugar-coating, Logan said, "Bad. He's not going to make it."

"But you don't know that," I said, knowing full well that he did. However, the kids didn't need to hear that.

We asked Abigail to call her vet, who arrived an hour later and gave the puppy a shot. He told the kids to just make Milo as comfortable as possible because he doubted the puppy would survive the night. I went outside with a blanket for Milo and watched as the kids talked to him in soft, soothing tones. I hadn't been standing there long when a huge bug, the size of a hummingbird, suddenly flew at my face. I swiftly swung my right hand up to protect my eyes and heard an ugly popping sound. A sharp, white-hot pain radiated outwards from my rotator cuff to the top of my arm, collar bone and neck. The entire area burned as though on fire. I knew that pain well, and I would deal with it as I had done the last few times my shoulder popped out of place—ignore it. The bone would eventually pop back in place. The pain, when it did, was even more excruciating. However, I hated the hospital, and I hated physical therapy even more.

As I lay in bed that night, I wondered what else could go wrong. I was sure Milo's cage had been locked. How had he gotten out? If the dog died, Michael would be devastated. "Why did this have to happen?" I cried out to God.

"Because people around them are going to start dying," He said.

My heart sank. The dog was going to die as God's way of introducing death to the kids. I started fretting about who was going to die, and prayed it wasn't Logan or me. I was miserable and in agony. I thought about rescheduling the baptism and then thought better of it. Despite the machinations of the devil meant to thwart God's plan, the baptism had to go on as scheduled, but the kids had to decide for themselves.

* * *

The next morning, I gathered them together. "Guys, do you still want to get baptized today? We can leave Milo with the vet and then pick him up when we come back. Or, I could call Pastor James and postpone. What do you want to do?" I asked.

"I want to get baptized today," Christine said.

"Me too," Nathan piped in.

Before Michael could answer, I held up my hand, stooped down so I could be at his level and said gently, "Before you say anything, take a minute to think about it. We don't have to do this today because I know you're feeling blue. Don't say yes just because Nathan and Chrissy said yes. If you say yes, make sure it's because you really want to."

Michael hugged me tight and whispered, "I want to."

"You're sure?" I asked.

I felt his head bob up and down enthusiastically in the crook of my neck and his small arms tighten around my shoulders. *"Take that, devil!"* I thought happily. "Ow, ow, ow, ow. Not so tight," I cried as my shoulder throbbed fiercely.

As we were leaving the next morning, I told Logan we were taking the dog to the vet, and then taking a trip with Abigail. When he asked where to, I told him the beach. Because we were going to be on the west end of the island, we had planned that after the baptism we would drive the extra half hour to Negril. Negril, which is on the coast, is well known for its Seven Mile Beach with beautiful turquoise waters and shallow bays. We hardly had occasion to visit, and so we wanted to make a day of it.

About twenty minutes into our journey, we spotted a police cruiser stopped ahead on the opposite side of the road. Two police officers stood outside the car dressed in red-seamed black trousers, striped light blue shirts and black peaked caps with red bands. One was pointing a radar gun. Our driver checked his speed, cruising steadily down the hill. Just as I thought we might be home free, one of the police officers stepped into the middle of the road and held up his hand. We were only detained for about five minutes while the officer verified the driver's documents, but it was five minutes too long. We were already running late because of Milo, and this could be the proverbial straw. I called Pastor James to explain, praying he would not postpone the baptism. To my utter disbelief, his car would not start, so he was running late himself. However, he assured me he was working on getting it fixed and would make the baptism whether or not it was. I shook my head, scoffing at the chutzpah of the devil. And he had called *my* persistence absurd?

We picked Pastor James up from his church because his car still was not operational by the time we got to Westmoreland. As we approached the river, Pastor James expressed his surprise at the river's emptiness. He explained that at that time of day, the river would usually be bustling with people bathing and laundering clothes. That wasn't a scene that was unfamiliar to me. In some small, rural communities, the residents rely on rivers as their main source of water as many of them don't have running water in their homes.

I scanned along the banks of the river, and there was no one in the water. It was eerily quiet. A lone onlooker sat on a nearby wall. We were close to the road and clearly visible to passers-by. A few people bustled about their business without as much as a glance in our direction. As we walked towards the river, my heart fluttered a little. This was it. The point of no return. I glanced over at the wall to see if the onlooker was still perched there. He was gone. I peered inside Abigail's SUV, then scanned the periphery of the property. The driver was also gone.

The area that Pastor James chose was a wider area that was somewhat like a pool. The water didn't rush by, but flowed gently, the movement hardly noticeable except for a few tiny ripples. Pastor James admitted that normally he would read a word of Scripture at this juncture, and then, the congregation would sing a few hymns or choruses. However, given that the situation was unique, he decided to dispense with the usual pomp and circumstance. He carefully climbed down the slippery, muddy incline into the water, and then extended his arm to help one of the kids.

I watched nervously as Nathan went in. I listened, as in answer to Pastor James' questions, he confidently affirmed his belief that Christ died on the cross for his sins, affirmed his faith in Christ as his personal Lord and Savior and affirmed the desire to be baptized in obedience to Christ's instruction. Pastor James then immersed him, baptizing him in the name of the Father, and in the name of Son and in the name of the Holy Ghost. As Nathan emerged, my heart swelled with joy. He had been bullied mercilessly at one school simply because he had an American accent, he was quiet, and he got good grades. However, he was quickly recognized by the students, teachers and staff at his new school as a kind, gentle soul.

The school nurse asked me once, "Where did you get Nathan?" When I frowned and asked her why she would ask such a question, she said, "Because he's not ordinary."

Nathan was always concerned with doing the will of God, even in the minutest of things. One day when I asked him why he constantly put others before himself, he said, "Because that is what I was born to do. I was born to suffer for the sake of others."

As Christine stepped into the water, I breathed a huge sigh of relief. I thought of how trying a time she had had, and I was grateful we were in this place—a place where all was still, except for the gentle banter of the wind with the leaves. It was fitting that she stood in a place where the water, unchlorinated, ran pure. No pollutants would touch her skin because, strangely, the usual visitors to the river had stayed home. What had kept them there? Had they heard something? Or, was it just an odd feeling that overcame them? I looked down at the water. It gently rippled and flowed by her, constantly replenishing the pool with fresh water. I was grateful we were in that moment—a moment where all else was forgotten, except what was well. As she went under the water, all that had happened to her was buried, and she rose up out of that water brand new.

As I watched Michael, my heart melted. He was only ten, but he was wise beyond his years and more courageous still. Whenever we discussed the things of God, he was very solemn. Sometimes I could only wonder what he was thinking. However, when he did speak, he spoke boldly and without apology. His fear of and reverence for God was unwavering. I wasn't at all surprised that he had chosen getting baptized over being with the puppy he loved dearly. As Michael's body broke the surface of the water, the leaves rustled softly in response to the caress of the wind. "Shhhhhh. Shhhhhhh," the wind whispered as though chiding the leaves to show reverence. A cool breeze passed over my skin, warming me, but I was not afraid. It was not the intense heat that engulfed me the night I sang at the crusade. Instead, I felt as though I had been enveloped by a blanket. As I stood there on what felt like hallowed ground, I knew that God had hugged me, and I felt unparalleled peace.

Lost in Translation

I dreamed that an angel came up to me and handed me a small piece of paper. On it was written the message: *Il est mort.*

Although there was no reference to the identity of the "he" mentioned, I immediately knew of whom the message spoke. It referred to Eustace. And, although my native tongue isn't French, I understood that the note read, "He is dead," thanks to the one French class I had taken in college.

"Do you want me to interpret?" the angel asked.

I shook my head vigorously. "No."

"Do you understand?" the angel asked.

I nodded. "Yes."

"Are you sure?"

"Yes," I confirmed firmly.

When I woke up, however, I was confused because Logan was on the phone to his dad. The message didn't say, "He is going to die." It said, "He is dead." So, how was Eustace alive? I realized then that what I had said yes to when the angel asked if I understood the message was the translation, not the interpretation. Funny, I didn't go to God. I decided to get to the bottom of it myself, so I inquired about Eustace's health when Logan got off the phone and learned that he had a serious illness for which he was receiving treatment. I thought that must be it then, and based on my own interpretation of the message, I surmised that Eustace would not get well. However, surprisingly he steadily improved and was eventually given a clean bill of health. And so, because God is a God of second chances, I surmised He had decided to give Eustace a chance. I told Eustace about the dream because I figured I got the message so that God would get the glory for sparing his life. Then, I just filed the entire thing away.

* * *

Roughly four years later and just two months before the kids were baptized, *I dreamed that Caleb and I were walking, and we came to a garden. To the back of the garden, there was a slipshod wooden stall that had various vegetables and fruits displayed. As we went further into the garden, I grew uneasy.*

"Caleb," I said glancing around nervously. "Let's go."

"I just want to see what they're selling back there," he said and continued walking.

I stood where I was, refusing to venture any further. The garden was overgrown with weeds, dark and eerie. The bushes I stood beside were lush and the peppers huge and lustrous; however, the vines were brown and shriveled. I hurried to the stall and said with urgency, "Caleb, let's go. We have to leave now!"

"Okay, okay," he said calmly as he turned to leave without buying anything.

"Something's not right about this place," I whispered.

Just then a young man appeared from what seemed like nowhere. He apparently was already in the garden because we were facing the exit, and nobody had come by us. He suddenly held up his right hand and blasted Caleb in his upper body. The force of the blast sent him flying backwards, and then he was gone. A door that had not been there before slammed shut, trapping Caleb.

"Noooo!" I screamed as I ran to the door.

I grasped the knob and pulled as hard as I could, tears running down my face. I began screaming, "God, please. Help me!"

I ran over to the young man and screamed, "Open the door!"

He just laughed. The menace rolling off him was almost tangible. It was choking me, but I refused to back down. I tried to punch him, but it was as though there were a forcefield around him. My blows were wild, meeting nothing but air.

I refused to give up and cried over and over, "God, please. Please, please, please . . ."

But my blows still did not find their target. I got angry and screamed, "God, why aren't you helping me?"

No answer.

The young man chuckled as he watched me claw and punch to no avail. Then, as if bored by the display, he began walking away.

He paused and scoffed, "You, I wouldn't even bother with."

He left, and I followed to see where he was going, leaving Caleb behind.

I called Colette that morning and told her about the dream. She was terrified, and I wondered if I had done the right thing. After I had given all the details, she cried, "Maybe it's not Caleb."

And there it was—my out. "Yeah. Maybe it's someone else, and I saw Caleb because dreams are like that. As the saying goes: Dreams don't walk straight." I had done my best to keep my voice on an even keel.

I knew in my heart, though, that that wasn't the case. I felt guilty that I had alluded to the ambiguity of dreams in lieu of simply speaking the truth. But I could not do it. Colette's voice had held such a desperate note of hope, it tugged extremely hard at my heartstrings. I told my kids and Abigail about the dream; however, Colette and I didn't talk about it after that, and I never mentioned it to Caleb or anyone else in my husband's family. I don't know how I would feel if someone came up to me and said I was going to die. Besides, chances were that Logan's family shared his sentiment regarding my dreams. I was troubled in the weeks that followed and quietly questioned God about the why of it.

* * *

I had another dream about a month after the first. *This time, I was on the shore of a body of water. Parts of the land were rocky, and the area was isolated and eerie. Everything was in black and white and varying shades of gray. Dark clouds loomed ominously over us. The trees in the swamp on the periphery appeared parched as though their roots were impervious to the water in which they were embedded. Sand, like ash, burned my feet. As I looked around, I fell ill at ease. Families were swimming, but my gaze fastened on one young woman in particular, who was in the water with two boys. As I watched, the water became troubled and black.*

I screamed, "Get out of the water! Get out of the water!"

People started swimming to the shore, but the woman with the two boys made no move to get out. I attempted to run towards the water. However, I didn't even get to take a step because out of nowhere, several beasts appeared, cornering me. They were huge although they came only up to about my knees. Their raised, sinewy shoulders caused the front of their bodies to be considerably higher and disproportionately larger than the back. They were hideous and appeared to be a mixture of various ferocious creatures. Their massive jaws housed two sets of uneven, razor-sharp teeth. They snarled and snapped at me, but I did not let fear deter me. I stopped focusing on the beasts and began shouting once again for the woman to get out of the water. I sighed in relief as she started swimming towards the shore with both boys on their backs, one tucked under each arm.

I could see she was tired, so I yelled, "Keep swimming! You can do it!" over and over until my throat was raw.

She swam for a while, but I could tell she was getting tired. She slowed gradually until she stopped.

Then, she just let one of the boys go.

"What are you doing?" I screamed. "You have to save them both."

I watched in horror as the boy slowly slid under the water and disappeared. The woman resumed swimming. My pleas for her to turn back fell on deaf ears. I sobbed uncontrollably, turned my eyes heavenward, and screamed at God, "Why?"

He said simply, "One has to die so the other can live."

Those chilling words haunted me in the weeks that followed. I did not understand the dream, but I managed to convince myself, Colette, Abigail and the kids that the dream was an inconsequential nightmare. I did not go to God with it because I was afraid. The only reason I told anyone at all was "just in case."

* * *

Two weeks after the baptism, the kids and I left Milo at Abigail's house and went to visit my parents in Florida for the summer holidays. After we had been there only a few days, Abigail called while we were in a pet store buying toys for Milo. My heart sank as I watched Michael grin and squeeze a squishy toy. Milo was dead.

It was a long weekend. Nathan's and Christine's sadness was more so for their brother than for the puppy. Surprisingly, they didn't have to console him long. After a while, he was looking at pictures, watching videos and telling funny Milo jokes.

That Monday morning, Christine said to me, "Mom, whatever happens today, it's going to be okay."

"Okay," I said as she squeezed me tight, but thought, "*Okaaaay.*"

Around mid-afternoon, Abigail called me from Jamaica.

"Hey," I said cheerily.

She hesitated. "Hey." She had dragged the word out slowly. Her voice was deep and flat and held a note of solemnity.

I frowned. "Everything okay?"

She didn't answer right away, and my heart skipped a beat. "Jabez

. . . Jabez . . ."

"What is it?" I asked anxiously, my stomach in knots.

"I just heard that Caleb was shot."

"What?" I cried. The room began spinning, so I flopped down onto the bed. "When? How?"

"He was taking a deposit to the bank, and he was held up."

I felt numb. This was not happening. "Where was he shot? Is it bad?"

"I don't know. He was taken to the hospital. I've been trying to get information, but I haven't been able to. I'll call you as soon as I find out anything."

As I hung up, I was overcome with grief. I knew what Abigail's next call would be, but I wouldn't accept what I didn't know for certain. I had to hear the words.

I didn't even have to wait an hour. "Jabez . . ." Abigail said, then paused.

"Is Caleb okay?" I asked although I already knew.

"No. He didn't make it. I'm sorry."

My chest hurt and my eyes burned with unshed tears. "Where did he get shot?" I asked although I already knew.

"Somewhere in his torso, but I'm not sure exactly where. There was nothing the doctors could do because the bullet fragmented, causing a lot of damage." Abigail sighed. "And to think I saw him in the bank this morning."

I thought about the last time I saw Caleb. He had come by to say goodbye the night before the kids and I left for Florida. I hugged him and said, "See you when I get back." The tears I was struggling to keep at bay fell unchecked.

I had to tell my kids but couldn't bring myself to do it until later that night. Bar none, that was one of the hardest conversations I'd ever had.

"Guys," I said nervously, "I have something to tell you."

They all sat and waited patiently for me to speak, but I couldn't.

"Did something happen?" Christine asked.

I nodded, my heart pounding hard.

"Did someone die?"

I nodded.

"What?" they asked in chorus.

"Is it Dad?" Nathan asked, his voice thick with panic.

"No," I said.

"Is it Uncle Caleb?" Christine asked.

My throat went dry, my heart pounded even harder, and I thought I might stop breathing. "Yes," I whispered.

"What? Was he shot?" Nathan asked.

I nodded.

Questions came for details I could not give because I only knew what Abigail had told. I had tried unsuccessfully to reach the family. Christine and Nathan openly expressed their shock, anger and then grief while Michael just watched—silent. After a while, he asked softly, "Is Uncle Caleb in a better place?"

My throat ached as I fought back tears. "Yes. He's in the best place."

"Are you sure?"

"Yes," I whispered, the pain in my throat unbearable.

"How will you know?"

"I'll know," I said firmly, placing a reassuring hand on his shoulder.

"Are you sure?"

"Yes, I'm sure," I said softly, but with as much conviction as I could muster.

"Okay," he said looking relieved. "So, there's hope."

"Yes, there is."

"Good. Can I please go to bed now?" he asked softly.

I hugged him tight. "Sure, baby."

Without another word, he left the room.

Despite the turmoil of the days that followed, Michael's response was what strengthened all of us. For the most part, he listened quietly to our conversations. The rare times he did speak of his uncle were never tinged with sadness, but with fondness. While Nathan and Christine had shown obvious purpose early on, Michael had not. All he had demonstrated as yet was a warrior-like constitution, not in a physical sense, but in a steely pragmatism that he often used to bring about calm in times of panic.

* * *

A few nights before Caleb's funeral, God woke me up. I kind of grumbled, "Lord, what do you want to tell me?"

He said, "Get up."

I opened my eyes reluctantly but didn't move.

"Can you please just tell me, so I can go back to sleep?" I groaned, covering my ears with my arms.

"Pick up the Bible," He commanded.

Well—I had to get up to do that.

"Open it."

And I did.

I didn't flip through it. I just opened it once and the passage before me was Matthew 8: 18-22. It tells of a disciple who asked Jesus if he could first go and bury his father before going with Jesus. To which Jesus replied, "Follow me, and let the dead bury their own dead" (NIV).

I was puzzled. "What are you trying to tell me?"

"Let the dead bury their dead," God replied.

And I understood. This is was about the funeral.

My heart sank. "I can't *not* go to the funeral. That's my husband's brother. He's family. I have to go," I pleaded.

My protest fell on deaf ears. I got no further response. In the time it took for me to fall back to sleep, I managed to convince myself that

God must have meant this command for another time.

I spent the next day lamenting about the impossibility of God's command. Although what happened was not easy to forget, it was easy to ignore as I busied myself preparing to do my part at the funeral.

* * *

I was uneasy as I entered the chapel. I hated funerals. Caleb's casket had been placed near the main entrance. It was open and would remain that way for a period for those who wished to view his body. I held my head straight and stiffened my shoulders as I walked past Caleb's casket. As I busied myself trying to find a seat, Caleb's daughter Danica came over. "Hi Auntie Jaye," she smiled, greeting me warmly.

"Hey," I said, trying to return the smile, but try as I may, I could not. Instead, I hugged her tightly.

"Did you go look at Daddy?" she asked.

I shook my head. "Nope, and I don't intend to."

She seemed a bit taken aback. "You sure?" she asked.

"Dani, I can't," I pleaded. "I really can't."

"I'll go with you," she coaxed gently. "It's your last chance because the casket is going to be closed soon."

I hesitated briefly, then agreed, "Okay." I held her hand tightly, and we made our way to the entrance of the chapel.

The closer I got to the casket, the tighter my chest became. As I looked down at Caleb's lifeless body, I was suddenly eleven again, and I was staring down at the still, cold body of my cousin. It was too much for me. I buried my head in the crook of Danica's neck, and she wrapped her arms tightly around me. She shushed me gently as tears violently racked my body. It took a little while and great effort, but I managed to calm and listen to Danica talk about Caleb's outfit. As she spoke, she reached into the casket and smoothed the lapel of his coat. I caught a sudden movement out of the corner of my eye and looked up to see Eustace's gaunt face.

"Don't disturb him!" he snapped angrily, glaring at Danica. She startled, quickly removing her hand.

I grabbed her hand, dragging her behind me, "Come on," I said and made my way to the front of the church. I glanced back quickly, taking one last look at Caleb. I thought of the last words he had spoken to me, "Take care of yourself. See you when you get back." I had to fight hard to keep from falling apart.

I busied myself for the duration of the viewing by running a sound check with Caleb's son, Justin, for the piano duet we were going to play. Nathan made sure the projector was set up to display the words of our song. The first part of the service was a blur. When Justin was called up, I took my seat at the keyboard next to him. My heart galloped as we played Whiz Khalifa's "See You Again." I barely managed to get through the song. I had to keep glancing at Justin's hands to cue myself on where I was in the song.

As I was making my way back to my seat, I felt unsteady.

As I passed Colette's seat, she gently pulled me into a squat and asked, "You okay?"

My vision was blurry. "No," I whispered.

"Take her outside," I heard her tell someone.

I felt hands on me as I was led outside and put to sit. I could hear fussing around me and then someone said, "Move back and give her space."

Then someone took my hand and felt my pulse. After a while, I heard a woman say, "Something's not right." Then fingers were placed on my pulse again. "Go get the doctor," she cried urgently.

My eyes began to gradually dim. I was swallowed up by blackness as I felt myself begin to travel. I felt like I was on a bad roller coaster ride, but without the turns and twists. I just shot forward, further and further into the darkness. I freaked.

"Oh God!" I begged, *"Please. Don't let me die here!"*

It was as if the rollercoaster stopped abruptly, only to shoot backwards. I felt myself flying backwards through the darkness until the darkness gave way to light. I could hear people talking again, and the worried faces of my family came into focus. I was still sitting up in the chair.

From Danica's account, as I sat there in the chair, my eyes held a blank stare, and I was unresponsive. She said she thought I was going to die, so she went to get some ice-cold water for me—not sure how she thought that would help—but as she approached my chair, she accidentally spilled it down the back of my dress. As soon as she did that, I jerked and became aware.

Instructions were given for me to be taken to the infirmary. My blood pressure was very low, and my heart rate was slow. I spent the rest of the service being monitored and cared for by a doctor there.

* * *

That night, as I mulled over the day's events, I remembered the night God woke me up and admonished me to let the dead bury their dead. I knew that that had something to do with what had happened to me at the funeral. However, I still tried to explain it away. Maybe it was exhaustion. Maybe it was anxiety. Maybe I was simply overcome with grief.

The next day, Abigail called me to find out about the funeral. She had not gone because of what I had told her about the night God woke me up. We chatted a little about how everybody was doing.

Then she said, "Something strange happened yesterday. I was at the kitchen sink when I heard God say, "When I say let the dead bury their dead, do you know what that means?""

I went cold all over. I asked what time that was, and she told me. It coincided with the time of my incident. I could no longer discount it as mere coincidence. This was confirmation that what happened to me was as a result of my disobedience. I told her then what had happened to me at the service. She listened impatiently, trying hard to contain herself, occasionally injecting an exclamation.

After I was done, she said firmly, "You should not have gone."

"I know," I wailed, "But how could I not have? Caleb was family. How could I explain not going? How would that look? Plus, Justin was counting on me. We practiced his song together, and I couldn't leave him in the lurch. The kids needed me to be there, and I needed me to be there."

"That's the problem. You cannot put your feelings or other people's feelings over what God has told you."

"I know, but in this case, I just couldn't do it!"

"Lord have mercy!" She had stressed each word. "Do you know what God just said? He just said, "The love of man is far greater than the fear of God."

I gasped, cold sweat washing my body. My heart thumped in my head as raw fear overcame me. "Oh my God, oh my God," I whispered rather loudly.

"Listen, Jabez . . . You should not have gone. No matter what God asks of us, we have to obey or suffer the consequences."

I was extremely penitent. I prayed for forgiveness and thanked God for being so merciful even though I was blatantly disobedient.

* * *

For months after the funeral, I was in a daze. One night as I lay in bed —sad after having talked to the kids about their uncle's death—I said to God, "I know everything is your will, but you could have saved Caleb if you wanted to. I asked for your help. I called out to you. I begged you for help, and you did not answer me."

"But I did," came the reply.

"No, you didn't," I bemoaned. "I screamed and begged, but you didn't help me."

"Yes, I did. When the door closed, Caleb died on the spot."

My heart raced, "What?"

"I heard you, and that's why he lived for a little while."

"What?" I asked incredulously.

My thoughts raced back to the garden and how the door closed never to reopen, and I understood. That closed door signified finality. The instant of the blast signified the last time Caleb would be seen alive. The fact that he did not die on the spot was purely an act of Divine Mercy.

Those who were around Caleb in the short moments before his death recounted how concerned he was, not for himself, but for his family. He prayed constantly, and as he neared the end of his journey, he asked God to receive him into His Kingdom. The manner in which he spent the last of the time he was allotted strongly affected those who bore witness.

I closed my eyes, and in an instant, I was outside the church a few nights before the funeral. I zoomed in on the indifference plastered on Eustace's face as he read the eulogy I had written at Colette's behest. He then tossed it between the front seats of his car, slamming the door shut on it forever. I remembered how disappointed I was because that eulogy spoke more to the essence of who Caleb was than the one that was actually read. I thought of my favorite line: "The measure of a Godly man is not what he does for others to see, but what he does when he thinks no one is watching."

My thoughts then sped up as if someone had hit a fast-forward button, and I was sitting on my bed reading my Bible. The words seemed to jump out from the page, "Let the dead bury their dead." I lingered here. "But how can people who are dead do anything?" I asked.

God said, "Those that are physically dead cannot."

Understanding immediately dawned on me. God was referring to the spiritually dead.

Suddenly, I was standing in front of the angel in my dream, being handed a piece of paper. As I stared down at the words "Il est mort," the angel asked, "Do you understand?"

Almost instantly, I was back at the casket standing beside my father-in-law. "Oh my God," I gasped and opened my eyes.

Got Ears

While I had had a few dreams about impending death, I also had dreams of comfort, hope, promise, guidance, caution, challenge, chastisement, and instruction. Over the years, these dreams facilitated my journey and deviation from what would be considered the "normal" course of things and led to my being described as divergent in a noncomplimentary sort of way by people who don't take kindly to "different."

My struggle to always obey God is what Jamaicans refer to as "haad eayz" (hard-ears). This expression has nothing to do with the ear's ability to perceive sound but with the refusal of the person hearing to obey. I often justified acting contrary to God's will because what He asked was too hard, wasn't in keeping with what I wanted, or simply made me uneasy. The cost of disobeying God is great, which He demonstrated at Caleb's funeral; however, the cost of obeying God can be equally as great.

I waited about a month after Caleb's funeral to talk to Logan about the baptism. I reasoned it would be easier and so not worth the drama if I just didn't tell him at all. However, I knew better. I approached Logan while he was having a bath, which was highly strategic. "Hey," I said nervously, sitting on the lid of the toilet. "I need to talk to you about the kids' baptism."

"Yeah. The baptism at Hope Springs is coming up, so they have to talk to Pastor," Logan said, somewhat distracted.

"No, they don't," I said, my heart thumping hard.

"Yes, they do. They didn't do all the classes, so Pastor is going to want them to complete the course before the baptism," Logan said quite firmly. He resented my contradicting him.

"Well, they can't be baptized . . . because . . . because they've already been baptized," I had rushed the last part of the sentence, getting it out before I choked on it.

"What?" Logan shouted, standing in the bath. "You better tell me you're joking."

"I'm not," I said my voice quavering. "They got baptized before they left for Florida."

"Who baptized them?" he yelled.

Was he serious? I scowled and shouted back, "Why are you asking who baptized them? Logan, don't pretend that we didn't have several conversations about how the kids were to be baptized. I told you God said that they had to be baptized by Pastor James. I also told you it had to be in open water, not at Hope Springs in a chlorinated pool and most definitely not by Pastor."

Logan looked at me his eyes hard and cold, his face blatantly displaying his contempt. "You are a wicked, wicked woman. And all this talk about God telling you to baptize the kids? I don't believe that. You don't even go to church. Besides, God doesn't talk to people now like He used to. It's not God you're hearing. Your messages are from the devil."

I gasped. "How could you say that? Is the devil going to tell me to go baptize the kids? How does that benefit him? When they got baptized, they were identifying with Christ. Listen to yourself. How can you say God doesn't talk to people like He used to? He's the same God. He talks to me a lot in my dreams—"

Logan butted in, his voice forceful, "Don't even mention your dreams. God doesn't talk to people in their dreams anymore. That avenue is what the devil now uses. This is the problem with you. You always have these ridiculous notions you know full well don't make sense, yet you say them all serious-like. It's either you think I'm stupid, or you actually believe what you're saying because you're in some kind of cult. Are you in a cult?"

I shook my head slowly in disbelief, outhaling loudly on a huge sigh. "Are you kidding? Just because God doesn't talk to you, it doesn't mean He doesn't talk to other people. Why are you limiting God? He can do and does do whatever He wants, however He wants, whenever He wants, using whomever He wants."

Logan's body shivered, maybe from the cold air on his damp skin or maybe from his rage. I wasn't sure which. "We're done. You went behind my back and baptized the kids without my permission," he said, his glare intense. "We're done."

I wasn't deterred. "You couldn't know the date because you would have stopped the baptism, and the baptism could not be stopped," I said, quite matter-of-fact. "I'm sorry you're upset, but I'm not going to apologize for doing something God told me to do."

Seething, Logan barked, "Get out and close the door behind you." He sat down as I got up to leave.

I paused, my hand on the doorknob. "Don't pretend as though I never talked to you about this, Logan. I even came to you for Pastor James' number and you told me to ask Lowell. What did you think I was asking for the number for? I told you the kids could only be baptized one way. You could not be there because you were disobedient and chose to go against God. You have one person to blame for that." I gently, but quickly, closed the door behind me before he could respond. I had to clasp my hands to quell the violent shaking.

The pit feeling in my stomach worsened with every step I took. Maybe I should have just contacted Pastor James and gotten the kids baptized without saying anything at all to Logan—end of story. I couldn't, though, because the baptism had been a test in obedience for all of us, including Pastor James. What happened with Logan was similar to instances in the Bible when God gave special instructions for a change of route or maintenance of silence if His plan was in jeopardy of being thwarted. Knowing this, however, did not make me feel any better.

That night, Logan came to bed, but he did not say a word to me. He lay on the far side of the bed, presenting me with his back. Just as he had done to me many times when I was upset, I pressed up against his back and hugged him. Logan flung my hand off and bolted out of bed. As I listened to his footfall on the wooden stairs and then heard the downstairs guest bedroom door slam, tears pooled in my eyes, stinging painfully. My heart ached as intense pressure built up in my chest. Relief came only when the tears finally slid down my face.

* * *

For many weeks following, my home felt like the frigid cold of Antarctica had sucked all the warmth from it. Logan remained either distant or combative. There was no middle ground.

One night, I said something—not sure what—and Logan flew into a rage, backing me up against the kitchen sink. With his nose almost touching mine, he screamed angrily in my face. I was terrified. I had only seen him this mad once before. I didn't want to let on how scared I was, but I was never adept at playing Poker. Wide-eyed, I squeezed my back up against the hard counter, attempting to create even an infinitesimal distance between us. It was useless as Logan only leaned in further.

I screamed at him, "Get the @&%# out of my face." My use of colorful language was always effective in jolting Logan. It was like throwing a bucket of ice water in his face.

He backed away from me but continued his rant. Wanting to get some distance between us, I stormed off and headed upstairs. I heard Logan stomping up the stairs behind me. I glanced over my shoulder and gasped. He was taking the stairs two at a time, quickly gaining on me. I dashed inside my bedroom and spun around to close the door, but Logan pushed hard against it, forcing me back. The door banged loudly against the wall, then swung back towards me a little. I rushed over to the bed and grabbed my cell phone.

Logan's face twisted with rage. "What are you doing with your phone? Are you planning on recording me?" he barked.

My heart raced, and I struggled to breathe properly. Intense fright and asthma do not good bedfellows make, but getting to my pump was not my priority. "Leave me alone, Logan!" I cried desperately.

I had to get to the kitchen. It was the best place to be if I needed to defend myself. Sidestepping Logan, I hurried downstairs. I hoped that he would give up, but he was hot on my heels. As I neared the kitchen, I glanced back nervously. I didn't see Logan. I figured he had gone into the guest bedroom. Relieved, I turned back, heading for the stairs. I needed to lock myself in my room until Logan either calmed down or left the house. Just as I got to the bottom step, I caught a movement out of the corner of my eye.

I spun around as Logan crowded me, holding his phone up extremely close to my face. "You're not the only one who can record," he snarled.

I turned away, but he quickly moved around me to stand on the step, blocking my access to the staircase. I tried to get around him, but when I moved to one side of the step, Logan moved over and blocked me. When I moved to the other side, he slid over to block me there as well. I gave up and just stood still staring at him. Seeming to lose interest, he moved off the step, but as he passed me, he brought the phone back up to my face. I held on to the top of it and pushed it down below my chin.

"Stop that, Logan. This is crazy. I wasn't recording you," I cried, my voice tinged more with frustration than with fear.

Logan reached back and—with tremendous force—swung his right fist forward and across his body, connecting with my right shoulder. I felt intense pain, and then the area went numb.

"What the @&%#? I can't believe you just hit me," I screamed, glaring at him.

Logan did not respond. Instead—kudos to his Shotokan sensei—he crouched into a fighting stance, form perfect, face wildly intense. "Come nuh," he taunted, jerking his fingers in a gesture meant to urge me to retaliate.

"Leave me alone!" I screamed.

Logan refolded his fists and danced around, lightly shifting his weight from one foot to the next as if he were Muhammed Ali. As I watched in disbelief, I thought, *"Oh my God. Who is this man?"*

"You're crazy," I yelled and began turning to leave. However, before I could move off, Logan struck out—much like a snake would—with a quick, sharp jab to the same shoulder. I cried out in agony as my shoulder throbbed, catching fire.

"Dad, what are you doing?" Nathan yelled from the landing.

I used that distraction as an opening to dash upstairs. "Mom, what's going on? I just saw Dad hit you. Are you okay?" he said, looking perturbed.

I nodded, not trusting myself to speak. The pain in my shoulder was beyond unbearable. Logan bounded up the stairs. "Your mother hit me first," he said with much conviction.

"No, she didn't," Nathan said, glowering at Logan.

"Yes, she did. I was only trying to protect myself," Logan insisted. His voice held a note of desperation. He needed Nathan to believe him.

"Dad, I saw what happened," Nathan cried, pursing his lips as he tried to control his anger.

"She was trying to steal my phone," Logan yelled.

Nathan harrumphed and slowly shook his head. "Dad, which is it? First, she hit you. Then, she was trying to steal your phone? Make up your mind," Nathan said sternly, his eyes hard.

"Fine," Logan huffed, turning to go downstairs. "Side with your mother."

In a firm, authoritative voice, Nathan said quite loudly, "Men are fools, and that's why men will die."

A chill ran up my spine. *"Which teenager speaks like that?"* I marveled, aware of the answer before I even asked the question. *None.*

Logan stopped dead in his tracks. Filled with unbridled rage, he marched over to Nathan. I thought he might throttle him. Instead, he came nose to nose with his son. "Are you a man?" he yelled in Nathan's face.

Nathan did not flinch. "Are you?" he asked calmly, but his disdain was palpable.

Logan stormed off, slamming the door as he exited the house.

To say things were tense in the house after that would be a gross understatement. For about two weeks, Logan walked around like a lion with a thorn in his paw. He left before anybody in the house woke up and came home only after he thought everybody was asleep. I suspected that when he wasn't at home, he was at his parents'. It was amazing to me that his parents would not encourage their grown son to come home to his family.

* * *

I decided to talk to Eustace and Constance about the situation because it was untenable. When I got to their house, Eustace was busy, so Constance and I sat in the family room and engaged in small talk. Every few minutes, Constance leaned over to massage one of her calves. Without any prompting from me, she launched into details I really had no interest in hearing. I took in the display of photographs, the tucks and pleats of the drapery, the sinking and yellowing of the old piano keys—and then I heard it, an urging to rub her leg.

"What?" I said to God, totally shocked. I glanced at Constance's face and then down at her leg. *"I'm not rubbing her leg,"* I said defiantly, my contempt building the more Constance talked.

Again, I heard, "Rub her leg."

"*This cannot be happening. This has to be a joke,*" I thought in disbelief. I had an aversion to touch, especially if it involved someone I was not particularly fond of . . . and this was Constance.

A third time I heard, "Rub her leg."

Every time God told me something a third time, it invariably felt like I was on my final strike. Not wanting to find out what the penalty was for striking out, I jumped into action. "Do you have something that you usually rub it with," I asked.

"Yes, a liniment," she said, still massaging her leg.

"I'll rub it for you," I offered.

Constance suddenly stopped rubbing her leg and studied my face intently. "That's okay. Eustace will rub it later." As if on cue, Eustace entered the room.

"*Not good,*" I thought. "*I have to get her to consent.*"

Eustace, who was chewing on a stick of sugarcane, held up a bowl to me. I didn't want sugarcane. I wasn't there to socialize. I had come about my business. Reluctantly, I took two sticks just so as not to offend. My darn face. I had to fix my face. As I worked my jaw out on the hard piece of stalk, I also worked on fixing my face. By the time I was done, I was able to muster a slight smile while I said, "I'll rub your leg for you. I really don't mind. Besides, I'm probably going to be here a while anyway."

Constance hesitated mere seconds and then said, "Okay."

I was thrilled. I knew all about missed opportunity. I had experienced time and again how displeasing that was to God. As I rubbed Constance's leg, it was like I was also rubbing away my contempt. Her relief became my relief. I was no longer on the warpath, primed for battle. I was ready to simply talk.

Constance and Eustace decided to hold the meeting in their bedroom because Constance was tired. She propped herself up on the bed, I sat in a chair nearby and Eustace sat on a hassock in the far corner of the room nearest to the closet. As I gave a synopsis of the situation,

Constance struggled to remain quiet. Then, in a spirit of feigned ignorance and impartiality, Constance said in a soft mellifluous voice, "Just so you know, Jabez, I don't interfere in my children's marriages."

I had to refrain from rolling my eyes. However, she must have seen a flicker of incredulity there because although I hadn't said a word, she felt the need to convince me. "Well, it's true. I stay out of your business and leave you people to live your own lives. However, we agreed to meet you because we wouldn't like to know we could have helped, and we didn't." When I remained quiet still, she asked, "Why do you think Logan is behaving this way?"

"How should I know?" I asked, frowning. Did she want me to psychoanalyze her son? If any theorizing was to be done, she was the one to do it. She held the counseling degree.

Eustace fidgeted on the hassock. I had forgotten him there. "What did you do?" he asked in a deep authoritative voice, stressing the word "you."

My blood pressure shot up. He could not be asking what I thought he was asking. "What do you mean?"

"Exactly that. What did you do?" He slightly paused between each word of the question as if I were obtuse. "You know, some women will box a man in his face, record his reaction and then put it up on YouTube to destroy his reputation and garner sympathy." What was Eustace talking about? When I looked at him as though he had two heads and a horn, he asked, "Why did you get your phone?"

Aha! Appalled, I said a little louder than I would be proud of later, "I did not slap Logan in his face. That's ridiculous! Do you know why I got my phone? Because I was afraid of your son and thought I might have to call for help. YouTube? Are you kidding me? I don't know the first thing about how to put a video up on YouTube. When you ask me what I did, that question implies that Logan's actions can somehow be justified. There is no justification for violence. It doesn't matter what I did or didn't do."

Constance butted in, "Logan doesn't get dinner when he comes home in the evenings because you refuse to cook. On top of that, he has to wash his own clothes?"

This was surreal. I must have crossed over into the twilight zone. I snickered and shook my head. We were now talking about—of all things—food and laundry. "I don't know what Logan has been telling you, but he has dinner to eat every evening if he so chooses, but he simply doesn't choose. As we speak, there are several plates of food—untouched in the fridge—that I'm going to have to eat myself or eventually throw away. And, even if I'm unable to cook because I'm bedridden, Abigail does . . . or I get takeout. Every time I'm doing laundry and I ask Logan for his clothes, he tells me he'll wash them himself. What am I supposed to do? Hold a gun to his head and order him to hand them over? These are quite the accusations coming from someone who minds her own business," I said heatedly, glaring at Constance.

"What about the swearing?" she hammered away, not missing a beat.

"What? I bet you heard I'm the only one who swears," I laughed. "Well, I'll leave Logan to confess his own sins. Truth is, when I am backed into a corner, I swear to get Logan to back off. I don't swear at Logan as a habit."

"That's disrespectful and very wrong," Eustace said firmly.

My blood reached boiling. "You can say whatever you want, but I cannot fight Logan. As skinny as he is, he's extremely strong. What do you suggest then? That the next time Logan has me backed into a corner or against the sink, I reach for a knife instead?" I heard Constance gasp, but I ignored her, glaring at Eustace.

"No, I'm not saying that. It's just that swearing accomplishes nothing," he said calmly, trying to pacify me.

"Why is Logan sleeping downstairs?" Constance asked, her tone accusatory. The sugary sweetness with which she had started the conversation long gone.

"Wow! You sure do know a lot," I sneered. "It's like you're a fly on the wall or something. You need to ask Logan that. I'm not a mind reader. I know why he went downstairs initially, but I have no clue why he's still there." Enumerating, I held up a finger for each point. "One, Logan left of his own accord. Two, I'm not going to beg him to come back. And three, the door is not locked."

Constance slowly smoothed the folds of her housedress, pressing her hands hard against her thighs as though she were fighting for restraint. "When you guys were to be married, I held my tongue . . . All I can say to you now, Miss Jabez, is that you better be good to my son," she warned, her voice steely. Although the use of the title "Miss" is meant to show respect, when an elderly person uses it in that tone, it is meant to show contempt.

I stiffened. "Do you think my parents would say that your son has been good to me? Truth be told, I have been extremely good to your son because he is not in jail. But . . . tell you what . . . the next time your son puts his hands on me, I'm calling the police," I said, my voice hard as granite.

Both Eustace and Constance remained quiet. In the small community we were in—and with their standing in society—that call would be extremely scandalous. Eustace's role as an elder of Hope Springs Eternal Missionary Church, businessman, Justice of the Peace, chairman of several prestigious institutions and organizations, and once Acting Custos Rotulorum of his parish meant that he was in the spotlight a lot. He was sometimes in the newspaper and on T.V. and probably had the numbers of several VIPs on speed dial.

Constance recovered first. "The baptism. What about that?" she asked, her voice like acid. She just was not giving up. "Don't you think Logan deserved to be at the kids' baptism? You went to a pastor of a different denomination, you deceived him, and got him to baptize the kids behind Logan's back. Pastor James didn't know that Logan knew nothing of the baptism. He said that if he had been aware, he would not have baptized the kids."

"You talked to Pastor James?" I yelled, as I leaned forward and braced my hands against the arms of the chair.

"Logan talked to him. Imagine his shock when he found out that you used him. There are rules, and you can't just pick up and baptize the children wherever you please," she yelled back.

My mouth dropped. Crazy must run in this family. I tried to count to ten, but only got to two. "I bet Logan didn't tell you that I talked to him about the kids' baptism several times and asked him for Pastor James' number. I deceived no one. I explained to Pastor James that God had chosen him to baptize the kids, and he obeyed God's command, without reservation, because he is a God-fearing man."

Eustace spoke up from his place in the corner. "Baptism is something that we look forward to in my family. My father was at mine, I was at Logan's and Logan expected to be there for his kids'. It's a rite of passage—something we look forward to and celebrate by taking pictures and preparing a special meal. We haven't even seen any of the pictures." His voice was weighted with his disappointment.

"That's because there are none," I said dryly.

"You need to apologize to Logan," Constance said emphatically.

I shook my head vigorously, "I will apologize for a multitude of ills, but I will not apologize for that. When I stand before God at Judgement, do you think I can tell Him that I disobeyed Him to please Logan or the two of you? Who is man to think that he is bigger than God?"

It was as though I hadn't spoken. Constance shouted, "What about the kids, huh? The kids are hardly coming to church. I want my grandchildren in church beside me—"

"I'm done," I said, equally as forcefully. I could not listen to anymore. I stood up abruptly. "I don't know why I thought you could be impartial . . . but before I leave, let me tell you a dream I had about you years ago but was afraid to tell you."

I re-took my seat and looked Constance square in the eye. "I dreamed that I saw Eustace waiting by a car outside a building that was under construction. I said hi to him but did not stop to talk. When I entered the building, there were workmen inside rendering the walls. You were supervising and being extremely persnickety. Things had to be done exactly the way you wanted, or they would have to be done again. I watched for a while until I heard God say, "Walk to the back of the room." I walked away, unnoticed, and kept going until I came to an opening in the wall to my left. I stopped. God said, "Look around the corner." I leaned forward and peeked down a long dark passageway. Then, He asked the question, "What do you see?" To which I replied, "Nothing." Then I heard God say, "Exactly.""

"What's that supposed to mean?" she asked, her brow deeply furrowing.

Without even so much as a tiny drop of maliciousness, I said, "You'll have to seek God concerning that." I stood up, looked from one to the other and said, "It was a mistake for me to have come here." I headed out the door and back into the family room.

Just as I was putting my shoes back on, Eustace called out, "Wait, Jabez." I looked up to see him with Constance in tow. "We want to say a word of prayer before you leave."

I agreed, but I really wasn't thrilled. All I wanted to do was get out of there to escape the dense, suffocating tension in the air. During the prayer, I blocked out everything Eustace was saying. Instead, I took in the display of old greeting cards on the entrance table, the busy pattern of the rug beneath the coffee table, the lines and grooves etched in the wood of the T.V. stand . . . When the prayer ended, I made a hasty retreat, barely muttering my goodbyes.

As I was about to get into my car, I heard God say, "Go back and hug them." I could not believe it. Although I was reluctant, I did not hesitate. I wasn't about to repeat my earlier blunder. Eustace opened the door, his surprise at seeing me written all over his face. He stepped aside. I felt awkward and really uncomfortable. "I just came back to thank you for your time," I said, hugging Constance first and then Eustace. As I hugged each of them, I felt at peace.

On the ride home, I asked God, "What was the lesson here?"

"There was no lesson. This was a test," He said.

"What test?" I asked really confused.

"You told me that you forgave Constance, but I am not interested in what you say," He said.

I once asked Logan to whom Jesus was referring when he used the word "neighbor." My hostility and reluctance to show Constance compassion were not characteristic of love. That God asked me to go back and hug them both after I felt unfairly ganged up on was like getting a bonus challenge on a test. The love of God is not a mere concept. It is visible, tangible and very real, and it is what facilitates forgiveness. That night, I truly forgave Constance.

* * *

Forgiving Logan, on the other hand, would take considerably more time—and that's the thing about deep-seated feelings. They are the interwoven threads of the noose in which one puts her neck. About a week and a half after my conversation with Constance and Eustace, I got a message from God for Logan, which I was very eager to deliver because it was one of reproach. Smugly, I delivered the message, but his response set me off. I rebuked him for his unfavorable response. Then, I pulled a "by the way," using the opportunity, while I had his attention, to light into him about some of our personal issues. But they turned out to be solely my issues because, as usual, Logan had no clue what I was talking about. His response was: deflect, deflect, deflect— which angered, but in no way deterred me. Although I basically got nowhere, I stormed off feeling satisfied that I had at least spoken my piece.

Not quite five minutes later, I received a phone call from Abigail. I had scarcely said hello when she asked frantically, "What did you do?"

I was stupefied. "What?" I searched quickly through my database and drew a blank. "What are you talking about?"

"What did you do?" she asked once more, her words forceful.

My heart started galloping. Her urgency frightened me. "What do you mean what did I do?"

"I was here making Daniel's bed when I heard God say, "Tell her not to use me!""

Oh. My. Heart.

I know for sure that after receiving countless jarring jolts like the ones coursing through it at that moment, my heart—at autopsy—is bound to be in extremely deplorable condition. No words. I had no words. But ears? I got those.

"Oh, God. I am so so sorry," I immediately cried out from a place deep in my heart.

"Hello?" Abigail's voice sliced through the silence. "Jaye?" She waited.

I sighed heavily. "You are not going to believe what just happened," I began, my heart tachycardic.

Real Me

Who is "Me"? There's the Me I perceive myself to be. There's the Me I project for others to see. Then there's the Me that God sees—Real Me. While it is possible to deceive man, it is impossible to deceive God. For years, I unintentionally deceived my own self, unaware that I was being untrue. I thought I was basically a good person, so I tried to portray that image to others, desperate for them to see me the way I saw myself. The Me I projected for others to see was generally affable, benevolent, gentle, compassionate, patient, considerate, humble and most times sincere.

The Me I perceived myself to be was as giving and forgiving as any wife could possibly be. I was a saint for forgiving Logan's transgressions way more times than I thought he deserved. He had far exceeded his seventy times seven quota and was riding on the coattail of grace. The Me I was portraying myself to be was loving and tolerant. I was the ever-supportive wife, never complaining to my friends or family about what I was going through. Whenever one of them called to my attention something Logan was doing and asked if I wasn't bothered by it, I feigned indifference. Then, God fact-checked me.

One night, *I dreamed I was in a void. The space was all white, sans windows or doors. In front of me, on a large table, were some gifts in small rectangular boxes wrapped in red gift paper.*

God said to me, "Pick one out for Logan."

I walked over to the table and picked up a gift. The price tag was $191.99. "This is too expensive for Logan. He doesn't deserve this," I *muttered, putting the box back.*

I took up another gift with a price tag of $191.25. "Still too expensive," I complained, putting it back and picking up yet another.

Dissatisfied, I replaced that one as well and picked up another. I kept this up for a while . . .$191.60 . . . $191.32 . . . $191.78 . . . Exasperated, I put it back and picked up one with a tag of $191.11. "Still too expensive," I grumbled.

Just as I leaned over to put it back, God said sternly, "No. Not so. You do not give to Logan because of who Logan is, you give to Logan because of who I am."

I recoiled, immediately chastised.

Ignorance can certainly be bliss because I was mortified at the realization that God saw me in that unfavorable a light. However, as I reflected on the dream, I realized how truly petty and unforgiving I was. Whatever was supposed to be given freely was weighted by conditions and came with and at a price. Because Logan never apologized for anything, I would accept gestures for apologies. The most predictable of gestures came by way of an oversized, imported Cadbury milk chocolate bar, which would be chock full of fruits and nuts if he was really, *really* sorry. As long as Logan was being decent, then I would be decent. However, my resentment at not hearing the words, "I'm sorry," would manifest in a subtle jab here or snide remark there—often masked in the weightlessness of harmless banter.

* * *

Because of the issues I had with my parents when I was growing up, for years I harbored feelings of anger and resentment toward them. However, by the time we were in college, my mom wrote my sisters and me to apologize, and I forgave her everything. I have had a pretty good relationship with my mom over the years. With my dad, however, no issues have been discussed and resolved. The Me I perceived myself to be was longsuffering, so I told myself I could get along with him no matter what. As such, I overlooked a lot of things that would probably cause confrontations if I thought about them. One day, while I was discussing my father, I said that despite the feelings I had towards him, if something should happen to him, I wouldn't step over him. The Me I was portraying myself to be was unfazed by anything my father said and did. But God fact-checked me.

I dreamed that both my parents were at a restaurant. The VIP section—where my mom was seated—was chicly decorated, creating a great ambiance. My dad, however, was seated at a table in a nondescript, poorly lit area in the back. I catered to my mom's every whim, doting on her. I indifferently glanced back at my dad a few times making no move to check on him or help him in any way. Each time I got the urge to check on him, I quashed it. Whenever I began to feel a twinge of guilt, I busied myself even more with my mother. Even when it was apparent she was satisfied, I still indulged her, insisting she order more. I even left and went to a patisserie to get my mother's favorite cake. Then, I went to another establishment to get ice-cream. As I made my way back to my mother's seat, I quickly glanced at my father, shrugged and thought, "Meh. Looks fine to me."

As I later pondered the dream, I thought it funny that although I knew I had underlying resentment issues, I was oblivious to their depth because they were hidden under copious layers of flake. On the surface, my dad and I had great rapport. He was a talker and so was I, so sometimes we spent hours in each other's company. Because of this, I always thought the feelings I harbored towards my dad would not affect my ability to care for him should the need arise, but I was delusional. If I were to be totally honest, there never was a question in my mind that should my mom become unable to care for herself, she would live with me. The few times I thought about what I would do with my dad should the same happen to him, placement in a nursing home was the only feasible option. However, I convinced myself it had nothing to do with how I felt about him and everything to do with manageability of care.

* * *

The Me I perceived myself to be was easy going and unfazed by what other people thought or did, and that's the Me I was projecting for others to see. Truth be told, I was actually hot-tempered—something I'd struggled with since childhood. At home, I could not express my anger even when I had been punished or I was displeased about something. I was always told to "fix my face," so I learned to hide. That spelled disaster, though, because when I could not contain that anger, it spilled forth. And out of my mouth flowed lava.

I seldom passed two in a count to ten. Once when I was ranting about something and feeling quite justified because I had been provoked, my daughter said to me, "Mom, you cannot fight fire with fire. God says you only get a bigger fire." That gave me pause.

Although Romans 12:18 admonishes that we live peaceably with all men as much as it depends on us (NKJV), I never felt it depended on me. What was customary for me was to stoke a fire until it became a raging inferno because I needed to be right, respected, and most importantly, understood. That meant never backing down from any fight even if it meant I would inevitably combust. I had believed for years that as long as I had good cause, I could say my piece until God "fact-checked" me, not in one, but in four dreams—and twice in one of them!

In one dream, I was at a formal gathering minding my own business. I didn't feel up to socializing, so I headed for a sofa. Before I could sit, Eustace approached me and—without saying a word—threw a glass of wine in my face and down the front of my dress. I was stunned. I looked around the room, and all eyes were on me. Some people seemed disapproving, but others whispered and hid snickers behind their palms. I was mortified. I grabbed the material and pulled it away from my skin while looking around for something to dab it with. Eustace looked at me and sneered, really smug. Then, he turned to walk away. Before he could get to the edge of the sofa, I grabbed the stopper of a decanter and threw it, hitting him hard in the back of the head. He went down with a thud. As a crowd gathered around him, I escaped into the kitchen. I grabbed a dishtowel, dabbed frantically at my dress, and tried to compose myself.

Abigail came in dressed in a serving tunic. She cleared her tray of empty wine glasses, poured more wine and began refilling her tray. She glanced at me and calmly said, "You should not have done that."

"Did you see what he did to me?" I asked, incredulous.

She did not respond. Instead, she picked up her tray and started for the door. She paused. "God says He is very displeased with you. It's not what people do to you; it's your response. You have to learn to control your temper, or you will be punished."

Without waiting for the retort I had at the tip of my tongue, she left the kitchen.

I often got hung up on what was done to me. Whenever someone hurt me, it was the hardest thing to let go. Long after the offense, I would repeatedly replay the details, chiding myself for not being faster on the draw, for not being the one with the better biting retorts or snappier comebacks. However, God was warning in this dream that He expects me to just let stuff roll off my back.

* * *

In another dream, I found myself on a crowded street amidst a throng of people in a religious parade. I felt boxed in, and I started to panic. I fought my way through the tightly packed bodies, going against the directional flow of the crowd. I eventually managed to break free of the crowd, but my relief was short lived. Coming towards me was another throng of people led by a priest. Rather annoyed, I approached them, determined to push my way through. As I got closer, the priest glared at me, held up his hand and shouted, "Go back! You're going the wrong way!"

Scowling, I yelled, "Let me pass."

His face brightened several shades of red. "You have no respect for authority. How dare you challenge me? Turn around at once!"

Rage rolled off me in waves. The priest reached out and roughly grabbed my arm. He immediately stopped speaking. His face—a concoction of terror and pain—contorted gruesomely. And then he fell. Members of his entourage immediately rushed to his aid. He was carried to a small, all-glass building with only one room and was quarantined there. Shocked, I stood with feet planted firm for a few minutes. Then, I hurried towards a window.

Upon seeing me, the priest screamed, "Keep her away from me!"

I rapped on the glass, and a monk standing right by the window glanced over his shoulder at me. Then, he turned around and spoke to the priest, but the priest was transfixed. He shook with terror— oblivious to anyone or anything but me—as he repeated many times over, "Get away from me! Get away from me . . ."

The monk opened the window and said firmly, "Please leave."

"I was just checking to—" The window slammed shut firmly in my face "—see if I can help," I finished softly.

Dissuaded, I sighed and turned around to leave. As I was about to step away from the building, a door opened, and two monks exited.

"Excuse me," the younger called out to me. "May we talk to you for a second please?"

I waited.

"We need your help," they both said at once.

The younger paused and the elder continued. "When you . . ." He cleared his throat. "When His Eminence fell ill, he was on his way to pray for a woman who is dying. Can you please come pray for her?"

Taken aback I said, "I'm sorry. I can't." Were they crazy?

The younger, livid, raised his voice and tersely said, "But you have to. This is your fault."

Without taking his gaze off me, the elder touched the younger's arm gently, quietening him. "You don't understand. Because of what you did, the woman will die. You must right this wrong by praying for her."

I was about to protest.

He held up his hand. "Before you say anything . . . It has to be you, no one else."

I could not have a woman's death on my conscience. I sighed and reluctantly agreed.

When we got to the sick woman's house, the monks removed their sandals and entered. I stopped short. They turned around and looked at me quizzically.

"I'm not coming in," I said.

The younger gasped, his mouth gaping open in disbelief. I ignored him and addressed the elder. "I can pray for her from out here."

The elder opened his mouth to speak and then abruptly closed it. He looked contemplatively at me and then said, "Are you sure?"

"Yes. I can pray for her from here."

He nodded and then turned to go inside. The younger glared at me briefly and then—cutting his eyes at me—he walked off, following the elder. I held my right hand towards the house and whispered a prayer of healing for the woman inside.

I waited . . . and waited. After what seemed like forever, the elder came to the door, his face solemn. "Thank you," he said softly.

I was anxious. "Is she well?"

He nodded. "Yes, she is well."

As I turned to walk away, the elder said, "Wait."

I stopped and faced him. "Oh, Lord. What now?" I thought.

"Everything you do has consequences. Your rage set off a chain

reaction and because of that someone almost died. That would have altered the course of things, which is not for you to do."

As I hung my head in shame, I heard a soft click. The monk had closed the door in my face.

This dream admonished me for being quick to anger. Going from "zero to one hundred real quick"—as Drake so aptly puts it—leaves no room for rational thought. Acting on raw emotion often has serious, and sometimes dire, consequences. I had to try to get past two in the count to ten . . . and better yet, learn to walk away.

* * *

In one dream, a group of us were holed up in a safe house. We each had tasks to do. Some people were inside the house, but Abigail and I were in the garage. While I packed supplies, Abigail busied herself at a sewing machine. After a while, I heard a commotion outside. Then, fists began banging against the garage door as angry voices demanded to be let in.

I looked over at Abigail, but she continued to sew, ignoring the interlopers. Annoyed I asked, "Don't you hear the noise, Abby? How can you just sit there?"

Abigail did not respond.

I raised my voice. "Aren't you going to do anything about it?"

She glanced up briefly. "No," she said and continued sewing.

The banging grew more intense. Agitated, I opened the garage door. Mobs stormed the garage seizing control of the house. Because of me, our safe house was no longer safe, and we could no longer stay there. Two angels came to move the group of us to safety. They instructed us to face forward and not speak, no matter what we saw. As we walked in between rows of buildings, I picked up on a menacing vibe. Two types of energy were being emitted within the walls—human and supernatural. I grew increasingly uncomfortable. The angels did not acknowledge the entities. Instead, they reminded us to keep looking forward and not speak. When we got to the next street, supernatural beings snarled and hissed at us while people jeered and made threats. The taunts infuriated me, but the other members of the group just kept walking, their faces stoic.

I turned to them and asked, "Am I the only one seeing them?"

Nobody responded.

"Am I the only one hearing them?" I asked.

Still, I got no reply.

I was extremely agitated. "How can you people act as if they're not there?" I yelled.

Nobody would even look at, much less answer me.

I turned towards the buildings and screamed, "Stop! Leave us alone!" The noise got louder. "Shut up and leave us alone. I rebuke you in the name of the Lord."

The angels didn't react to my tirade—nor did anyone in the group. When we cleared the buildings and got to an open area, a booming voice—from a small speaker box perched in a tree—angrily addressed me, "What have you done? You've killed them all!"

Dread gripped me. "What? What do you mean?" I glanced around but did not see the angels nor the rest of my group. I looked back up into the tree. "What do you mean?" I asked frantically.

My only reply was deafening silence.

This dream reminded me that sometimes the best course of action is to do nothing—hard as that may be. God is saying that I need to trust that He will always take care of me. He sent two angels! What more could I have asked for? It has always been hard to ignore the threats around me and be totally trusting and vulnerable. I have been in fighting mode since I was young, and I don't know any other way to be. However, there is "a time to be silent and a time to speak" (Ecclesiastes 3:7, NIV)—which I should be careful to heed—especially when God is giving the orders.

* * *

In the final dream, I was at home when I heard a knock. Wrapped in a bath towel, I opened the door to find my father standing there. I made no move to let him in because he was the last person I wanted to see.

"Can I come in?" he asked.

I hesitated. "Uhm . . ."

My father continued, oblivious to my reaction to his presence. "It's not just me. I have a few of my friends with me and we're hungry. What do you have to eat?"

I rolled my eyes and grumbled irritably, "That's too bad because I have nothing here to give you to eat."

He chuckled. "Come on. You can make us something."

I frowned and ground out, "What do you mean make you something? Are you kidding me? I'm busy. You can't just show up whenever you feel like without calling. And, as if that's not bad enough, you brought friends?"

"But we're not going to stay long. As soon as we're done eating, we'll leave."

I sighed. "Daddy, I have to go," I said impatiently and shut the door, none too gently, in his face.

I marched into the bathroom, grumbling to myself. I stood in front of the mirror and recoiled at my reflection. Several black veins on the left side of my face, near my mouth, visibly bulged under my skin. They snaked like tiny vines—diverging in myriad directions away from my mouth—and traveled up my face towards my left temple. As I watched in horror, the flesh on the left side of my lips began to rot. The rot slowly decimated my lips—following the path of the veins—to travel up my cheeks. Small black veins became visible on the right side of my face as the contagion began to spread there. Too frightened to watch anymore, I jumped out of my sleep.

This dream admonished me for being unkind, uncompassionate

and too quick to speak. As it is in the physical realm, I don't hide my feelings. Most times, I just let my anger fly. In this dream, however, it was more like irritation—different side of the same coin. And that's the problem, looking at sin in varying degrees. It would be ideal for me if God categorized sin: irrational, irate behavior—first-degree anger; grumpy irritation—second-degree anger; wicked, wicked thoughts—third-degree anger. However, anger is anger. James 3:6 (NIV) speaks of the tongue as a fire that corrupts the whole body and sets the course of one's life on fire. My tongue has been my greatest weapon. It is powerful, causes great damage and is extremely hard for me to control. However, the fallout from the use of that weapon can have dire consequences. According to Proverbs 18:21(NIV), "The tongue has the power of life and death." That is why God keeps cautioning me to control mine because not only will others suffer from its misuse, so will I.

* * *

By man's standard, I'm a fairly good person, but that's not the standard by which I will be measured at Judgement. While man looks at my outward appearance, God is only interested in the part of me that cannot be seen by others—the part that determines who I really am, my heart. It's one thing to be shown my faults, but revelation is pointless if it does not inspire change. What God asks of me is simple, but simple is often hard.

As I struggled with some of what God had revealed to me, He took me to the story of the rich young man in Mark 10: 17-22 (NIV) who got a shock when he asked Jesus what he should do to inherit eternal life. After rattling off a list consisting mostly of things that the young man should not do, Jesus told him the one thing he needed to do and that which he was lacking. He told the young man to exchange his earthly riches for heavenly treasure and then follow Him. The young man went away sad. Although the young man appeared to be doing what was right because he kept the commandments, that was not enough. He was unwilling to let go of what he had grown accustomed to and what he had come to value. The young man's riches signify whatever hinders a person.

For Me, it's anger, unkindness, unforgiveness, pettiness, vengefulness, arrogance, disobedience, recklessness, stubbornness and hatefulness. I have deleted "good" from the list of adjectives I use to describe myself. I've also put to death and buried the Me I perceived myself to be because the only Me I need to project for others to see is the Me I am constantly working on changing—Real Me.

La Petite Chance

I entered a banquet hall in a dream one night a few months after Caleb was buried. As soon as I passed through the doors, I was approached by a short, portly, dubious-looking man—obviously the host.

Jovially, the man said, "Welcome." Then, waving his hand towards a banquet table, he said, "Please. Eat."

I looked around nervously, but I didn't see anyone I knew. I looked back at the host. Something seemed really off about him, but I couldn't place what it was. "That's okay," I said rather quickly, needing to put some distance between us.

The man grinned widely. "Come on," he coaxed, placing a hand under my elbow and leading me towards the table. "There's plenty to choose from."

He stepped back a little and waved in the direction of the table. "Just help yourself."

I wavered for a split second but then held my ground. "No thanks."

He shrugged. "Suit yourself," he said with a smile his eyes did not reflect. Head held high, he strode off towards the entrance to greet the other arriving guests.

The table went on for what seemed like miles. In the center were long, rectangular aluminum containers that were about five feet long and about six inches deep. The ones close to me were filled with various meats like roast suckling pig, roast duck, baked ham, roast turkey, lobster, crab, roast beef and fish. Numerous platters of sides—close to *the edges of the table on both sides—sandwiched the meats. I strained to see further down the table.*

"Right this way," the voice of the host wafted across the room. I glanced around to see him approaching the table with Colette and Danica.

"Enjoy," he said pleasantly, a hand outstretched in the direction of the table.

I raised my hand slightly and waved discreetly, but neither Danica nor Colette looked in my direction. Instead, they both bent forward and buried their mouths in the rectangular containers and started eating. Eyes wide, I gasped as my hands flew up to cover my mouth. The cacophony they made was a loud, sloppy combination of slurping, snarling, chomping and grunting.

"God, what are they doing?" I whispered.

"Feeding from the trough," He replied.

Blindly, I backed away quickly from the table, bumping a few people in my haste to retreat.

I lay in bed that morning, very disturbed. I couldn't wipe from my mind the sight of Colette and Danica bent over the table, nor could I unhear the sounds they made as they partook of its offerings. "God, what was that?" I asked.

I got no explanation. Instead, He said, "Tell Danica I give every man a chance."

I walked around in a daze for most of the morning, not sure how to tell either one about the unflattering dream. I contemplated their reactions, worried I might offend or anger them. It took a few hours for me to come to my senses.

"What am I doing?" I thought, *"If I deliver this message, they might get vexed. If I don't deliver this message, God will definitely get vexed. Well . . . It's better they get vexed."*

I called Colette several times but was unsuccessful. Anxious, I eventually left a message—remembering to say the one thing that was sure to get her attention . . . "I had a dream." Sure enough, within a short time, my phone rang.

"Hey," she said, "are you calling about what happened to Danica?"

My heart galloped hard and fast. "What happened to Danica?"

"You haven't heard?" she asked in disbelief.

I became frantic. "No! What happened?"

"Danica and a friend were robbed at gunpoint while they were walking near the mall. Two men rode up on a motorbike, and the one on the back jumped off and demanded they hand over their money, laptops, phones, and jewelry. They took everything from them. The gunmen didn't hurt them although one of them got agitated when Danica's friend hesitated to hand over something he implored them wasn't his."

"What?" I shouted. "You mean something so serious happened and nobody told me?"

"I can't imagine that. I thought for sure you had heard." She sighed heavily. "Yes, my dear. You could have heard that they shot and killed my daughter."

"Oh my God. I know . . . and just months after Caleb was shot," I said, shaking my head in disbelief. "God is so good."

She agreed and then said eagerly, "Come. Tell me about the dream."

She listened intently as I recounted the details. She was quite taken aback and wanted to know what the dream meant. I assured her that I was as oblivious as she and encouraged her to earnestly seek God's guidance.

When I later told Danica the dream and relayed the message God had given me for her, she was shaken up. At first, she said she did not understand why God would portray her like that. However, after some introspection, she called to say she did. And that's all that mattered. That acknowledgment presented an opportunity for atonement.

Aha! That was what Pastor Hardy had meant about the onus being God's. I was simply the messenger, a conduit, a sure-fire way for a message to reach the intended recipient. I was in no way responsible for the content of the message, the reaction of the recipient, or the possibility of a particular outcome. No postman or woman ever stood around to see how I react to the mail I open.

* * *

Soon after, *I dreamed that I ran to my front door after hearing a commotion outside. I yanked the door open to see several supernatural beings—with white hair and unusual blue eyes—beating my husband with chains. The chains were very long, and the links were huge and thick. The beings were levitated several feet off the ground. Logan floated as well, but he was not as elevated as they. He was naked. I screamed as all their chains connected with his body at once. The beings swung with tremendous might, causing Logan to cry out. As he threw his chest out and bent his back, his head snapped backwards. His face wrenched in agony as tears ran down into his ears.*

"Noooo!" I cried and attempted to run outside, but I couldn't. There was a forcefield trapping me inside. I pushed against it, refusing to give up.

Logan straightened his back and brought his head upright, but he was unable to keep it up. His head lolled forward as if it was about to unhinge. The chains went high into the air and then came down with incredible force. Logan threw his head back and wailed.

"Stop!" I screamed, pushing harder against the invisible barricade.

Skin tore from Logan's flesh, and blood oozed from huge gashes. Tears poured down my face as I tried unsuccessfully to breach the forcefield. The chains went high into the air once again and then came down hard. Logan howled, his knees buckling—his limbs seemingly weightless—as his hands loosely flapped to and fro. His head fell so far back that it almost touched his behind. His body seemed as though it might snap in two.

"Noooo!" I screamed over and over until my throat was raw. Not once did the beings look at me.

I jerked awake, shaken and extremely troubled. It was one of the rare times I didn't question God—too afraid of the answer. I watched Logan keenly in the days that followed to see if there was anything amiss. However, I detected nothing. I couldn't go to Logan given his stance on my dreams, so I just had to wait and see.

* * *

About a month later, I got that I was to send my husband a message. At the time, I just wrote what I was told. However, I later realized the message was a combination of Galatians 6:7 and Hosea 8:7.

The message read:

Do not be deceived. God cannot be mocked. Whatever a man sows that is what he will reap. The man who sows to please his sinful nature will from that nature reap destruction. Sow the wind. Reap the whirlwind.

"Oh, Lord," I cried out, "Why? Those are fighting words!"

Not only did my husband not want to hear any of my dreams, but he had never been receptive to any message he'd gotten from God through me. Besides, because of our countless issues, I felt he would think that I was needling him. My pleadings fell on deaf ears. God continued urging me to send the message. This went on for hours until I finally relented. I sent the text, and as expected, I got no response. Every time Logan rejected one of my messages, I felt like a messenger shot.

When my husband came home, I asked, "Did you get a text from me today?"

He absentmindedly asked, "What text?"

Exasperated, I grabbed his phone from his hand. "Let me see that."

I impatiently searched his phone to find my message, and my heart stopped. On the screen—recorded mere minutes before my message was received—were seven messages that read:

Reap destruction.
Reap destruction.
Reap destruction.
Reap destruction.
Reap destruction.
Reap destruction.
Reap destruction.

I gasped. They were all sent from my number within a minute of each other. "What is this?" I asked no one in particular.

I ran to my bedroom and grabbed my phone. Just as I expected, none of the "Reap destruction" messages were there. The only sent message was the one I had sent. The first "Reap destruction" message had apparently been sent eight minutes before I even hit my "send" button. I immediately called the kids to show them both phones.

I kept saying over and over again. "I don't understand. I did not write this."

Nathan took both phones and after perusing the messages he said, "Mom, I don't know how this could have happened. The messages Dad got were from your number—but not your phone."

I quietly handed my husband his phone back, not mentioning anything to him. For weeks, I was stumped and shaken up. Realizing that you've failed God is incredibly disheartening. God should never have to beg me to do anything. I wasted all that time going back and forth—arguing with Him—behaving as though He needed me. He demonstrated quite plainly that if I am ever unwilling, He can do the job Himself.

* * *

In that same year, *I dreamed that I was standing at my gate when the wife of a former pastor of Hope Springs Eternal Missionary Church approached me. We greeted each other warmly, and then we stepped into my yard. We headed directly to the backyard, talking and laughing as we went. Then the pastor's wife gasped. I turned to see what she was staring at, and my mouth dropped. The clothesline was filled with Logan's clothes—only they were filthy and muddy. Several pieces of his garments had fallen off the line and were laying on the soggy, muddy ground. The pastor's wife immediately hurried to the line and started yanking down the dirty clothes, glancing around every once in a while to ensure that no one from the neighboring yards was watching.*

It was not a surprise to me that the dream alluded to shameful things that Logan would not want anybody outside our family to know. However, it was jolting to see a metaphorical concept represented in such a literal way. What was more interesting was that the person attempting to hide those things from public scrutiny was a member of the church. Given Logan's propensity for mendacity, I was not surprised at the volume of laundry. I'm sure there is a lot I don't know, and if Logan had his way, would never find out. I grew up hearing the expression, "Truth will out," and references being made to Luke 8:17 regarding secrets inevitably being revealed or brought to light one day. Seeing that manifested in a dream was actually remarkable.

* * *

I ran into Lowell in town one day. "Hi sis," he greeted me affectionately, and after asking after the kids said, "How are things going between you and Logan? I hope they've gotten better. I have been praying for you because the devil is going after marriages hard."

"Thanks, we need it," I said, happy to have someone in our corner. My expression turned somber as I said, "Things have actually gotten worse . . ." I told him about the hitting incident and the constant fights about women and money. As I spoke, Lowell was really expressive in his disapproval of Logan's behavior, shaking his head and interjecting an exclamation at strategic points.

I was hardly done speaking when Lowell said angrily, "But I don't understand Logan. What is this I'm hearing? This is the second time he's put his hands on you, which is unacceptable. He and I are going to have strong words."

While it sounded great, I doubted it would make a difference. His previous talk certainly had had no effect, but I couldn't bother pointing that out at the risk of coming across as a naysayer.

Lowell shook his head in disbelief. "Why do you have to split the bills fifty-fifty? My wife doesn't pay half our bills. As a matter of fact, I don't pressure her for any money. Taking care of my family is my responsibility. Logan shouldn't make you feel bad about what he does for his family. Boy, Logan a real *maama man*!" (Boy, Logan is a real murmur man) he sneered, his face taut.

I was really taken aback by his use of such a disparaging term to describe Logan. It was really over the top because to be called a *maama man* is a huge insult, and Lowell certainly would never use the term to Logan's face. *Maama man* is used to refer to a man who whines incessantly—like a woman—over trivialities.

I listened quietly while Lowell went on some more about how much of a *maama man* Logan was. Then, regaining his composure, Lowell said, "Don't worry. I'm going to deal with Logan because this can't go on." His voice held a note of promise.

* * *

I had to talk to Pastor James, but I could not reach him on his phone. I worried that he might be avoiding me because of the fuss Logan and his parents made about the baptism. Three days after my conversation with Lowell, I spotted Pastor James walking towards the Bible college where he was a lecturer. I prayed that I would be able to find a suitable place to pull off and turn around before he disappeared on me. When I got to the college, I was relieved to see his car still parked in the yard. As I approached him, my heart thumped erratically because I was nervous about the reception I would get.

"Jabez!" Pastor James said, a bright smile lighting up his entire face. I exhaled.

I hugged him warmly. "Hi, Pastor. I'm so happy I finally found you." It was hard to contain my excitement. "I came by a few times and left messages for you, but I never heard back."

"Yes . . . well . . . I must apologize for that. I've been having problems with that phone and had to get a new number."

"Do you have time to talk?" I asked, my fingers crossed. It had been several months since the baptism, and I was anxious to clear up any misunderstanding.

"I have a class now, but if you give me a few minutes, I will be able to talk to you," he said.

When he returned, I got right to the point. "Pastor, we need to talk about the baptism."

"Yes, we do. I got a call from Logan to say that he was unaware that you were going to baptize the children, and he was extremely upset. I'm really concerned about that." I listened, fighting hard not to interject. "Then, Brother Lowell called to confirm that you had indeed baptized the children behind Logan's back, you are not attending services, and you are actively speaking out against churches—"

I didn't hear anything after that, but I felt it—the knife that had been embedded, unnoticed, in my back for months. Lowell really had me fooled. His performance three days prior was well worth an Oscar.

I didn't let Pastor James finish. "Lowell?" I cried in disbelief.

"What does Lowell have to do with anything? Lowell actually called you?"

Pastor James frowned. "Yes, he did." The look on his face indicated he realized he was smack in the middle of an oh-oh moment. Confidentiality is paramount in his position as pastor, and I knew he would never intentionally betray anybody's confidence.

Yet I pressed. "When?" I asked, still reeling.

Pastor James looked a tad uncomfortable. "Several months ago."

I wanted to find out what else Lowell had said, but I didn't want to contribute further to the awkward position in which Pastor James had unwittingly found himself. I said, instead, "I can't believe this! But I shouldn't be surprised. Lowell and Logan have known each other since high school, and they are like brothers. Never mind that I've known Lowell longer; I guess men stick together. And speaking out against churches? I would never do that. I have never told a single person to leave the church, and I never will. I grew up in church and kept going— albeit reluctantly—until God called me out. Lowell has never heard me speak ill of the church, so I'm not sure where he's coming from with that." ·

What Lowell did to me, however, was not a priority. I had to clear the air where the baptism was concerned. I backtracked a bit to have Pastor James understand where I was coming from. I talked about some of my experiences: the appearance of the angel beside me at Hope Springs as I sang, why I stopped going to church, my dream predicting Caleb's death, and most important, what happened to me at the funeral because I disobeyed God. I spoke hurriedly, wanting to say as much as I could to make my case before Pastor James had to return to his students.

Pastor James listened intently, and his interest prodded me into giving more details than I had originally intended. I could have talked all night but decided to wrap up. "So, you see, God is working in phenomenal ways in my life. I cannot disobey a directive from Him because there are real-life consequences for me. I never hid my intentions from Logan. I told him the message from God just as I told it to you. However, he kept bringing up baptism at Hope Springs, and each time, I made my position unequivocally clear. The problem is he never took me seriously . . . oh, and by the way, I asked Logan for your number, and he told me to ask Lowell for it."

Pastor James raised his eyebrows at that. "Really?"

"Yes. Logan chose not to be a part of the baptism."

Pastor James said, "Wow! Jabez, after listening to you talk, I have no doubt that God speaks to you. It's obvious you and Logan are on different levels spiritually." He then glanced at his watch. "Jabez, unfortunately, I have to go back inside. Take my new number. You can call me tonight after class, and we can finish talking on my drive home."

As I drove home, my heart overflowed with the agony of betrayal and the sorrow of loss. My eyes welled with tears. I was not a mathematician, but I knew how to add two and two. All the information that Pastor Ellis had about my marriage had come from Lowell—not my mother-in-law as Colette had suspected. I felt like a fool.

Jeremiah asked, "Who can know the heart?" The answer is no one because "the heart is deceitful above all things, And desperately wicked" (Jeremiah 17:9, NKJV). Of all the wickedness I had encountered and all the struggles I had had with the people in my life, in that moment, no one's heart epitomized Jeremiah's description more aptly than Lowell's did. Not to say that what Lowell had done to me was the worst thing anyone could have ever done, but as Proverbs 14:10 (NIV) says, "Each heart knows its own bitterness." And my heart was bitter.

* * *

Not long after that, I was just a few houses down from Abigail's house when I got a vision of my husband lying on his back, unable to move. He had been made immobile in a car accident that killed his female companion. I had to be turning him to sponge him off as he was unable to help himself.

I snorted at the image and said, "Really, God? You must be joking! Should that happen, I'm going to go *Diary of a Mad Black Woman* on his behind." Well, I used the not-so-nice word for behind.

When I got to Abigail's house, she frantically ushered me into her study. She wore an expression of grave concern. The words tumbled quickly from her lips. "I just had a vision of Logan. He was lying in a bed made up with white sheets, and he could not move. You were sitting on the edge of the bed feeding him soup because he couldn't feed himself."

I gasped. My stomach somersaulted at the same time my heart sank. "What? How long ago did you get this?" I asked in disbelief.

"Just a while ago," she said, grimly.

"You're not going to believe this . . ." I began, relating the vision I had gotten on the way to her house and, abashed, I admitted my response.

Abigail's mouth dropped open. "My God! You got that on the way here?" Then her expression grew stern. "And your response was what? You know you can't do that!"

"I know," I admitted, my expression grim. I did not want to talk about me. I was in shock. This was beyond surreal. It's one thing to be shown something that will happen, but quite another for someone else to get that same thing—at that precise moment. Besides that, I really didn't have it in me to take care of Logan in that way. God was asking too much.

". . . be extremely hard." What? I hadn't heard a word Abigail had said. She gesticulated passionately. "But regardless of what has happened between you and your husband, God expects you to care for him because he is a part of you. You and your husband are one. You will have to put aside your feelings because it is not about you. It's God's will be done."

I was ashamed and deeply chastised. "I know. When I had that vision of me taking care of Logan, I was in shock. Why would God ask that of me after all that has happened? I'm not going to lie to you; it's going to be hard to set aside my feelings, but I'll do what God has asked of me when the time comes," I said, trying to convince not only Abigail, but myself as well.

Wanting to shift the attention from me and my shortcomings onto God's awesomeness, I said, "Isn't it crazy-cool that God showed the two of us the same thing at the same time?"

"Yes," she agreed, excitement lighting up her face. "God *is* crazy-cool."

We discussed the visions many times in the months that followed. Abigail had to constantly remind me, especially after an argument with my husband, of the importance of doing what God expected of me when the time came. I tried my best not to worry too much about the meaning of the vision. However, it was not easy to do.

* * *

In that same year, *I dreamed my husband approached me. He wasn't alone. A woman was with him. He waved some papers in my face, told me they were divorce papers, and demanded I sign them. When I told him I was going to do no such thing, the woman got in my face and screamed, "You need to sign them because I'm tired of hiding. We have a funeral to go to, and I want to be able to sit beside my man without tongues wagging. Sign the papers because I'm not hiding anymore."*

I leaned in even further until our noses almost touched and snarled, "Stay out of this! This is between my husband and me. You're a nonentity—a nobody—which means that you don't factor in this equation."

I turned to Logan and crushed the top half of the papers. "I'm not signing that—ever!" I yelled before storming off.

About two months after that dream, I was home one morning when a horn honked at the gate. Logan had been gone only five minutes. I thought maybe he had forgotten something. However, when I looked, I saw a car I didn't recognize. Reluctantly, I made my way to the gate because the driver was sure to have seen me since I'd opened the front door. I almost always ignored vehicles I couldn't identify. The driver called my name in the form of a question, and when I answered in the affirmative, he stuck his hand out his window and handed me papers.

"You've been served," he said flatly.

I frowned. "Served? With what?"

The man shook his head, a look of incredulity flashing across his face. "With divorce papers."

When I continued to stare blankly at him, he shook his head and said sympathetically, "Your husband is divorcing you."

I stood at the gate a while after he drove off, too shocked to move. Logan was divorcing me? After all that I had put up with over the years? I was the one with more grounds for divorce than I could count. And to do it in such an underhanded way? He could have at least given me a heads-up. What I could not admit in that moment was—if Logan's words and actions were indicators—I had been given tons of heads-up over the years, which I disregarded time and again because I was honor bound by two words, "till death." Not wanting to make a spectacle of myself should anyone happen by, I blindly made my way to the house through a haze of tears. Michael and Christine met me at the front door.

"Mom, who was that?" Michael asked, stepping back when he saw the tears running down my face.

"What's wrong?" he and Christine asked at once, their faces filled with concern.

I could hardly breathe, much less speak. It took a while to get the words out. "A man dropped these off for me. They're divorce papers. Your dad is divorcing me."

Michael looked at me quite sternly and asked, "Mom, why are you crying?" He stared at me, awaiting my response. However, I was so taken aback I could not speak.

Christine hugged me and said, "Hush, Mom. It's okay."

I called Nathan who—after getting over the initial shock—said calmly, "Mom, God showed you this would happen though, so why are you surprised?"

That statement calmed me. Nathan was right. I had been given the one heads-up that truly mattered. And suddenly, I wasn't so devastated. I looked at the petition then. I shook my head at the differences my husband had cited as grounds for the dissolution of our marriage: religion, value systems, family structure, finances. I actually laughed when I read the words "value systems." I skipped all the legalese and flipped to the last page of the document. There at the bottom were two signatures—my husband's, and that of the chief witness, Lowell Lovelace, Justice of the Peace.

Unlike in my dream, I did not plan on contesting the divorce. Logan and I had fought enough for a lifetime, and I was not going to fight anymore. Instead, I cried to God, "I can't handle this. You're going to have to deal with this. You said that whatever is broken is already fixed, so I'm taking you at your Word."

* * *

A few months later, *I dreamed that I sat on a bench in the waiting area of a hospital. My eyes were trained on a set of double glass doors, my body tense with anticipation. I saw a movement from the corner of my eye and turned my head to see a little girl—about ten years old—*

dressed in a white hospital gown. She smiled and sat down. I briefly glanced at her but then returned my focus to the double glass doors.

"Are you scared?" a soft voice asked from beside me. I turned to see the little girl carefully studying me.

"Yes," I replied honestly.

"Don't be scared," she said, her voice calm and reassuring. "He's not going to die."

I frowned. How could she possibly know that? She stretched out her hand and gave me a book. The title read, "La Petite Chance" which means small chance. Confused, I looked back up at her. We held each other's gaze, and then understanding dawned on me. This was about my husband and the chance that he would be given. Albeit a small chance, it was a chance, and that meant he would not die in the hospital. There was hope after all. I relaxed.

"Thanks," I said, holding her book out to her. However, she refused to take it.

She shook her head and rested a hand on it to brace it away from her. "No, keep it. It's yours."

I continued to push the book against her hand, "I can't keep your book."

She held firm—keeping the book in place—and said, "It's not mine. It is for you." She stood up and smiled. Then she turned and walked away.

Curious and awestruck, I got up to see where she was going. She walked down to the end of the hallway to meet another girl. This girl was older—maybe in her late teens. The older girl took her hand, and they walked out of sight around the corner.

That dream haunted me because it confirmed the visions of Logan that Abigail and I had had. I had been struggling tremendously with what had been shown to me. Regardless of the anger I felt toward my husband for giving up on our marriage almost as soon as it had begun, I didn't want anything to happen to him. I would rather he be somewhere without me than nowhere at all.

A few days later, my mom called me and said, "I had the strangest dream. I saw Logan, and he was lying in a bed. I had to be washing his chest and back because he was unable to help himself."

It took me a few moments to get over that shock. No matter how hard it was for me to accept what was to happen to Logan, I could not deny it because God had now confirmed it through two other people. This He did because He knew I would have a hard time accepting what I had been shown. By endeavoring to help me come to a place of acceptance, God showed me His heart for compassion and kindness and confirmed to me that He really does care.

* * *

A few short months later, *I dreamed I was at home. I ran into a bedroom and shouted to Abigail, tears running down my face, "They've come and taken him away!"*

I searched frantically for something to wear. I threw clothes all over the room, trying to find something suitable to wear. I was hysterical. "I don't know where they're taking him."

I fought to get dressed, fumbling in my urgency. I dragged on a pair of baggy, crushed shorts, which I struggled to pull up over my hips. I managed to clumsily drag a shirt over my head—able to get it only halfway down my torso. However, I didn't care. I rushed from the room and dashed through the front door. My yard was filled with observers—interlopers really. I didn't recognize anybody in the group of about fifty people and wondered, first off, how they had come to be there.

Then I saw my parents-in-law and thought, "That explains that." My only acknowledgment of my parents-in-law was a steely, fleeting glance, and then I ran past them up to my gate.

A hearse was just outside the gate. The driver was about to leave. I banged urgently on the driver's side window and begged, "Please.

Wait! I need to see my husband."

Hesitantly, the driver got out and opened the trunk door and there, lying on a gurney of sorts, was my husband. Tears rolled uncontrollably down my face as I bent and gently kissed his cheek. Although he looked as though he peacefully slumbered, his cheek was eerily chilled.

"Ma'am," the driver's voice jolted me. "I have to go now."

I begged, "Please, just a little longer."

He looked at me, a mix of pity and regret. "Ma'am, please."

I stepped away, and the driver slammed the door shut. I knew that that was the last time I was going to see my husband. Angry, I batted at my face, not wanting anybody to witness the tears which I thought evidenced my weakness. I marched through the gate, and as I passed my in-laws, I paused to glare at them. They glared back without saying a word. I whirled inside and slammed the door soundly behind me.

I woke up panicked and stayed awake for over an hour fretting on the dream. Then, I fell back into a fitful sleep. *This time, I found myself in a time prior to the hearse dream. My husband was alive and well. Thank God! I had to warn him. He was with a group of friends.*

I approached him and whispered, "I need to talk to you."

Annoyed, he said, "I'm busy."

He re-joined the conversation, ignoring me. However, undeterred, I refused to move. I waited impatiently, biting my tongue until I could no longer contain my frustration. I yanked on his shirttail insistently. "I really need to talk to you," I whispered.

He followed me reluctantly. "What is it?"

I struggled to form the urgent words. "I need to warn you. You're going to die. I've seen it. There are things in your life that you need to change before it's too late."

He scowled. "Don't come to me with any of that. I have told you over and over again that I don't want to hear any of your dreams. This is what you pulled me away from my friends for?" He glared at me, awaiting a response, and when none was forthcoming, he angrily stormed off.

"You need to listen to me!" I desperately shouted after him. But he kept going without as much as a backward glance.

Befuddled as to how to get Logan to listen, I went to Abigail's house. I hoped she would have the insight I lacked. I poured my heart out, my tears flowing freely. Abigail listened carefully, and then in a severe tone that did not match the stoic expression she wore, she asked, "Why did you do that?"

She paused briefly—not for me to answer but to take a deep breath—and then she continued, "God didn't give you a message for anybody. You can't take it upon yourself to try and save anyone. Everything is according to God's will, not your own. You really should not have done that."

As she talked, I cried a river, but she made no gesture of sympathy. Instead, she said to someone nearby, "Give Miss Jabez a plastic bag for her tissues." She waved at the mountain of tissue heaped on the sofa beside me.

I was hurt that she had scolded me instead of showing the compassion I thought I deserved. How had it all gone wrong? I was trying to stop a disaster. I could no longer stand to be in that dream. I was helpless, useless, powerless and apparently clueless.

I fought out of my sleep to find that I was covered in cold sweat, my heart thudding erratically. I had hours left before daylight and was determined to stay awake because I couldn't handle any more dreams.

After about a half an hour, however, I succumbed. *This time, I found myself in a time after the hearse dream. I was sitting, dressed in black, on a chair outside a church. Two men dressed in black suits were standing nearby.*

The tall man said to the shorter one, "Isn't that his wife?"

When the short man answered in the affirmative, the tall man then asked, "So, what is she doing outside?"

The short man just shrugged, and then they headed inside the church where the funeral service had already begun.

I made no move to go inside the church. I simply sat there. Alone.

These three dreams that I had back to back really put me in a funk. Even though I had gone back in time to try to save my husband in the one dream so as to influence all possible outcomes, there was no changing the course of things. I resolved, then, to put my feelings aside and do for Logan—without question or grumbling—exactly what God wanted me to do.

* * *

It was after I truly came to terms with what I had to do that *I dreamed I heard a persistent banging on my front door. I opened it to see a man I did not recognize standing there. "Didn't you hear it?" he asked excitedly.*

"Hear what?" I asked.

"The explosion last night," he said, looking at me strangely. "Everybody else heard it. How could you not have heard it? It was extremely loud."

He was getting on my nerves. "Well, I didn't hear anything. What happened?" I asked impatiently.

"There was a loud explosion in the middle of the night, and when we ran outside to see what had happened, we saw that one of the walls had come down," he said, pointing to the periphery of my yard. Where there were once two walls, one parallel to the other, stood a solitary wall. All that remained of the other were remnants strewn on the ground.

* * *

It has been roughly a year and a half since I saw my husband's death, and yet he lives; whereas, my cousin died the very night I saw his death, and Caleb died three months after I saw his. I am still alive almost nine years after I saw my death because of the extra time that I have been given. I never know exactly how long it will take for the fulfillment of something God has shown me, but that's not on me. If—like Hezekiah—God gave me an additional fifteen years, then a few years still remain. Until my time is up, I plan to make the best of the chance that I have been given. I hope Logan does the same.

The Valley

I had a series of strange dreams back to back that confused me. One, in particular, was pretty disturbing. This went on for about two weeks before I finally got an answer regarding the bizarre place I was visiting while I slept.

In one dream, I was in an old, decrepit hospital when an elderly woman came up to me. "I can't find my husband. Perchance have you seen him?" She wrung her wrinkled hands as she glanced around apparently distraught.

"What does he look like?" I asked. I don't know why I did that because no one had been my way the entire time I was seated there.

Her face lit up with love, admiration, and longing. She stared off as if transported to a place in which only the two of them existed. "He is tall, a handsome devil, with the sweetest of smiles and the kindest of eyes. He has a full head of wavy brown hair—untamed, unmanageable," she smiled, adding dreamily, "so soft."

Her expression changed, her mood becoming maudlin, as she returned her focus on me, her pale, gnarled fingers fretting with the folds of her long skirt. "He is a soldier and was injured in battle. I have been told mayhap he was taken here, but I can't find him anywhere." She glanced around, seemingly jittery.

"I'm sorry," I said.

"Thank you, child," she said absentmindedly, staring down the hall as though something had suddenly caught her attention. Then, without another word, she walked away.

I watched as she disappeared around a corner at the end of the corridor. My last thought before I woke up was, "How odd. Why is a dead woman looking for her husband?"

* * *

In another dream, I walked up to a fountain that was being choked by overgrown, dried-up vines that snaked into convoluted knots and coils, forming a well-armored, thorned cocoon. The water inside the fountain had dried up, leaving behind moss and darkly-stained concrete. I gasped. I had been here before. It was where I had been standing when Colette's nephew Rory approached me with a message. Only, then, the fountain had spurted jets of crystal, clear water that cascaded like showers of rain into the huge basin below. Vines of dark purple clematis flowers (dark eyes) had hugged the fountain's basin, stealthily creeping up its walls. The fountain looked dark and ominous now, and my skin prickled. I was being watched.

I hurried away from the fountain and ended up in a modern, well-equipped hospital. I entered a room where a small figure was partially reclined on what appeared to be an operating table. A huge light fixture, attached to an arm, hovered over the person's covered head. As I watched, the sheet fell off, and a young girl who was obviously dead came towards me. She was badly burned.

She stopped a few feet from me. "Help me," she begged, holding out both her charred hands.

I felt faint. "What happened to you?"

She started to cry. "My mother burned me." She inched further forward and begged, "Please help me."

I backed away, horrified. "I'm sorry. I can't help you."

I ran outside, looking for a way out. I saw a crowd going through a door. I followed suit, hoping the door would take me far, far away.

However, the space was cramped, and people were clawing, shoving and punching to make it to the front.

God said, "Go back."

I was beside myself. I couldn't go back because I would be right where I started. I stalled, trying to figure out a way forward, and then someone elbowed me. A fight broke out in front of me, and a man was shoved so hard that he staggered backwards, slamming into me. It was like being hit by a brick wall. I was packed in tight and struggling to breathe. Panic gripped me, and I desperately clawed my way out. As soon as I was back outside, God began guiding me. I kept following His instructions until I woke up.

* * *

In one dream, a well-known woman, with whom I had just performed a song, said as we left the stage, "This is my last performance."

That I could not imagine. Shocked, I asked, "Really? Why?"

She smiled, a far-away look in her eyes. "I've worked really hard and now I'm going to enjoy my life. I've earned it."

"I don't believe it." My mouth literally hung open.

She laughed and said, "Come on. I've got something to show you."

She kicked off her heels and stripped off her stockings. She dashed to the edge of the hill we were on, paused for a second to look at me, and then, with that huge, infectious laugh of hers, she bolted down the lush, grassy hillside. I dashed to the edge of the hill to see her running, both arms outstretched at her sides. She waved them up and down imitating an airplane, squealing in delight.

"Oh man," I muttered.

The only thing worse than walking in heels was barefooting it. I toed off my heels, peeled off my stockings and set off down the hillside. As my feet touched the grass, I felt a sharp pain and looked down. I was walking on weeds. As I looked over the slope she had just gone down, all I could see were rocks and weeds. What had happened to the grass? I painstakingly made my way to the bottom.

When I got there, however, her happy-go-lucky mood had changed to frenzy. She searched wildly among bushes and behind trees.

"What are you looking for?" I asked, concerned.

"My daughter!" she shouted at me. "Don't just stand there. Help me find her!"

I stood there gawking. "What?"

"Help me look," she said, parting some shrubs and peering through the opening she had made. "She was here, and now she's gone!"

I had no clue what was going on, but I began to search.

"I know who's responsible," she shouted angrily.

"Who?"

"Her father," she screamed. Her face twisted, not only in rage, but in fear and pain so strong, they were palpable.

Before I could remark, God firmly said to me, "You need to leave this place!" I immediately obeyed by forcing my eyes open.

* * *

In another dream, I found myself in an arena. I sat in the bleachers watching in horror as people choked, punched, stabbed, hacked, and maimed each other. A hideous, porky man, sitting a little too close to me, slapped his thighs and chuckled in delight. I spun around to glare at him in disgust.

"Why are you laughing? They're killing each other!" I yelled, incensed.

I thought he hadn't heard me as he continued to watch the attacks, egging the participants on. Then, he turned to me and said, "Yes. So they are."

"But that's crazy!"

"Look," he raised a grubby hand and pointed towards the field. "See that man? He killed his wife. That man killed a security guard. That woman drowned her children . . ."

The list was so long, I struggled to keep up. Plus, it was hard hearing over the screams and roars on the field.

I turned to look at him. "So, who killed the butcher?" I shouted.

He pointed. "The woman with the two left feet."

As he said that, a hush fell over the crowd. All eyes focused on me. It occurred to me then that despite the length and severity of the onslaughts, nobody had died. They all glared at me. They were bloody and battered. Some of them were missing limbs, had eyes that were hanging from their sockets, and sported weapons protruding from various parts of their bodies. Still, they were standing.

The fat man cackled. "Now you're going to die."

"What?"

He slapped his thighs, threw his head back and chortled. Then, he looked at me and said in a singsong, "They're going to kill you."

I gasped. "Why? I didn't do anything!"

He abruptly stopped laughing, leaned in closer to me, his eyes hard and cold. "You ask too many questions."

Dread gripped me as a hue and cry went up from the field, and then everyone moved all at once, marching towards the bleachers. I sat frozen, horrified. My heart galloped extremely fast, failing in its job to get blood pumping to my head. These people weren't going to get a chance to kill me. I was going to drop dead.

Just then, I heard God say, "You need to leave this place."

I shot up and looked around for the exit. "I don't know where to go. I don't know my way out!" I cried desperately.

God said, "Go up the steps."

As I got to the top, He said, "Go right."

I jumped out of my sleep.

I had a few more of these kinds of dreams, and every time I woke up, I felt sick and drained. My body felt as though I had been on an arduous journey, and my emotions were all over the place. I needed a break from the ominous and the obscure. I wanted narratives that included unicorns and posies—and I hate both.

I was feeling so overwhelmed that, one day, I asked, "God, where is this place that I go?"

"The Valley of the Shadow of Death," He said.

My chest caught fire, chilling my skin and raising my head off my body. That level of fright could not be good for a body.

My first thought was, *"I didn't just hear that!"*

My second thought was, *"Yes, I did."*

Then I thought, *"No I didn't. Maybe I thought I heard that . . . no . . . I did hear that! How can this be? I've never heard anyone say that that was a real place."*

I vacillated a while until I had my umpteenth thought, which was, *"This is crazy, but I have to accept that it is what it is because I couldn't make this up if I tried!"*

I contacted Pastor James, and after an "I'm not crazy" disclaimer, I told him a couple of the dreams as well as the answer I had received from God about where it is that I go.

He listened quietly.

"Have you ever heard anyone say that the Valley of the Shadow of Death is an actual place?" I asked.

"No," he said.

"What do you know the Valley of the Shadow of Death to be?" I asked, knowing full well he would not be substantiating what I was now certain of.

"Well, what I've always understood is that it is a metaphor for our trials and tribulations."

My heart sank. Not good enough.

Desperate, I asked, "You've never read anywhere that it's an actual place?"

"No, I haven't." His tone was matter-of-fact.

I wasn't giving up. "But it's an actual place in the spiritual realm. I've been there," I said passionately.

Calmly, but firmly, Pastor James said, "The bottom line, Jaye, is that you don't belong there. A child of God does not belong in a place like that."

Gut punch.

That bothered me immensely. Why was I going to the Valley? How did I end up there? How is it that I kept going back? What lesson was I supposed to learn? All these questions kept firing at me, and one day I was feeling such despair that I asked Pastor James to pray for me. All I said to him was that I was exhausted and wished I were somewhere else.

* * *

That night, *an angel came to me in a dream and warned me about spirits, naming the various kinds of spirits and what they do. It was a lot of information, so the angel warned, "Pay close attention and take note!"*

I tried to follow, but it was too much information. "Take note" must have been literal, so I grabbed pen and paper.

The angel said, "Regardless of their methods, ultimately, all of these spirits have the same goal. That goal is to distract you and keep you from your purpose." The angel explained that these adverse spirits can bring about unfavorable feelings: despair, self-loathing, anxiety, fear, among other things.

Then, the angel led me to a place that was built like a fortress. It was fortified with tall, strong brick walls, iron gates, and iron bars at the windows, and it contained hidden passageways and safe rooms. I recognized it as a place I had been before in another dream. Only, in the other dream, I was not led there, I was already there. The angel, in essence, was simply taking me back.

The angel warned, "Don't leave this place. Hide here. This is the only place you'll be safe." Then I was alone.

I was ecstatic. I had been saved from the Valley of the Shadow of Death! That morning, I messaged Pastor James to thank him for praying for me.

His reply:

> *Your life belongs to Christ. He paid for it with His. Surrender what is rightfully His to Him each day and live in purpose and freedom.*

I thanked him and said that I would. I included a smile emoticon but couldn't communicate further because I was busy.

Later that day, I messaged him saying that I had to explain why I had smiled earlier at the encouragement he gave me, and then I told him about the dream.

His response:

> *The Spirit of the Lord is pretty amazing!! I just spoke as I was led. Stay in that "secret place." Remember, he that dwells there shall abide under the shadow of the Almighty (Most High).*

I grinned, amazed. While I had discerned that the place to which the angel led me was metaphorical, I did not connect it to the stronghold mentioned in Psalm 91. I thought of Psalm 23, and how like David, I was never alone. God spurred me into leaving the Valley, and when I was lost, He guided my way. I was extremely comforted by that.

* * *

Whatever the Valley of the Shadow of Death is a metaphor for, one lesson is that God is ever with me regardless of the situations in which I find myself. David alluded to this in Psalm 139:7-8 (NKVJ) when he said, "Where can I go from Your Spirit? Or where can I flee from Your presence? If I ascend into Heaven, You are there; If I make my bed in hell, behold, You are there." It is comforting to know that whatever trials and tribulations I face in life, God is my refuge and my strength, a very present help in times of trouble (Psalm 46:1, NKJV).

It was never revealed to me what precipitated my visits to the Valley, but I told God I desired never to go back. The last time I left there, the gateway to the Valley closed permanently behind me.

And Stranger Still

I wasn't the only one having strange dreams. *Nathan dreamed he was walking outside when he heard a loud boom. He looked up to see an enormous clock in the sky. It ticked normally for a short while, and then the ticking sped up, much like a timer does before it stops. He watched people milling around, but no one seemed to have heard the explosion or noticed the ticking clock. They simply kept going—business as usual.*

For days, Nathan worried about the state of the world because he saw the dream as a warning that time was running out for people to get their lives in order before Christ returns.

Nathan's angst was made worse by another dream a few days later. *He dreamed that he stood by a window and watched as a great body of water rose in the distance. It towered above everything in its path, then barreled towards the house in which he stood, taking with it everything in its path. He stood riveted as everything was swallowed up: people, animals, buildings, trees, cars.*

Both Christine and Michael tried hard to calm Nathan. However, nothing seemed to work until Michael reminded him that when we die, we are not truly dead.

Not long after that, within months of each other, Nathan and I had dreams that were eerily connected. *In my dream, I trailed a young man to a cliff's edge. Evil rolled off him in suffocating waves. In the valley below, there was a multitude of people spread out as far as the eyes could see.*

The young man raised his arms and shouted, "Who's ready to be healed?"

The crowd went wild, and people raised their arms and screamed.

"Are you ready to be healed?" he shouted.

People became even more frenzied, flailing their arms and whipping their heads back and forth as they screamed in unison, "Yeaaaaah!"

I stayed hidden and watched in horror as the crowd got misled, knowing full well I could do nothing. His name wafted towards me on the wind, and I shivered, fear crawling up my back.

Although the dream was terrifying, I didn't hide it from the kids. I gave them the details, including the young man's name, which consisted of three letters. I did not describe him, however, as I did not want the kids visualizing him. I thought it would be less scary if they couldn't put an image to the name.

In Nathan's dream, the world was in chaos. The place was desolate. Many of the trees were dead—scorched by fire, buildings were flattened, and debris filled the streets. Many vehicles were overturned and mangled while others burned. Airplanes collided mid-air, causing fuselage and balls of fire to rain from the sky. There was pandemonium as people sought refuge from the minions of a maniacal young man seeking to kill them. We were also being hunted. However, every time we hid and were found, angels came to our defense. The young man became enraged at his minions' lack of success and would probably have offed us himself, except he could not come near us. Angry, he tramped away, laying waste to anything and everything in his path. Grass withered and died under his feet, birds fell dead from the sky as he walked under them, trees flamed as he walked by them, and people fell dead with a wave of his hand.

As Nathan relayed the dream, a chill ran up my spine. When he described the young man, my heart did several things hearts are not meant to do. His description matched that of the young man in my dream. I could not hide my terror. I gawked at Nathan. "That's the same man in my dream," I said breathily, whispering his name so softly I wasn't sure anybody heard it but me.

How could we have both seen the same person? I guess I should not have been at all surprised given the mountain dream Abigail and I had had. I looked at Michael, then at Christine. Christine was sitting perfectly still and staring dead ahead, as if in a trance. I began to pray, my insides roiling fiercely, *"God, please. Don't let the seizures be back. Please."*

"Christine," I called anxiously. She did not blink or move. "Chrissy," I called more forcefully. Still, she did not move.

"No, no, no, no," I thought. I didn't know what to do. I tried grabbing hold of myself. *"Think, think, think."*

Christine's seizures used to sometimes manifest as staring episodes in which her right hand would curve inward and stiffen. I looked at her hands. Neither was stiff, which was a good sign. Then, Christine slowly raised her right hand to eye level.

"Mom," Nathan whispered nervously. "What is she doing?"

I shrugged, not daring to take my eyes off Christine. She started writing in the air, using her index finger. We gasped simultaneously. What on earth was she doing? My stomach did a somersault—or maybe it was a backflip.

"Chrissy," I called softly, not wanting to startle her. However, she ignored me and kept writing.

As we watched with bated breath, she finally blinked, looked me dead in the eyes, and whispered, "6, 6, 6."

I gawked at her. Where had she gone? What had she seen? Between my heart, my stomach and my skin, I was not faring well. "What are you talking about?"

"His name is a number, and that number is 6, 6, 6," she said, very matter-of-fact. She was calm and did not appear frightened.

"Show me," I said eagerly although I already knew the truth of what she had just said. I had discerned his identity as I watched the crowd scream wildly in adoration of him, eagerly yearning for whatever ominous "miracle" he was offering to perform in their favor. However, I hadn't said, not wanting to scare the kids. Funny how that worked out.

Christine looked around for something to write on. "No," I said, gently resting a hand on her shoulder, staying her. "Write it on the wall." I'm not sure why I instructed her to do that, except for the niggling feeling I had that it should not be written where it would be visible.

Christine scooted over on the bed until her index finger touched the wall. She wrote the first letter of the young man's name, and then she changed it very easily into a six. The six looked as though it had been turned upside down and then flipped over on its backside. Next, she changed the second letter of his name. That six was right-side up but looked like it had been flipped over on its backside. Finally, she changed the last letter of his name. That six looked as though it had been turned upside down. Then, as we watched in awe, she held her hand as if the numbers were three dimensional. She slowly turned and flipped the numbers until each was set aright.

"The Beast," I whispered in amazement as I watched the pieces of the puzzle fit. To have had an idea of or feeling about something, and then have that confirmed in such an unusual way, was indescribable.

"What?" Nathan cried, placing his hands on his head. "This is weird. Do you know that?" he said to no one in particular. Then, he began whispering over and over, "Oh my God. This is crazy."

Michael, however, was very quiet. I searched his face for signs of fear, but I saw none. Michael was most times hard to read, which was disconcerting in instances like these. "You okay?" I asked him, and he nodded wordlessly.

We talked about the dreams and Christine's revelation for a while. Nathan spoke the most, shuddering as he repeatedly relived the horrifying events of his dream. I just let him talk because while I had not seen the destruction, I had seen the man, and that had been enough to terrify me. After that night, we never spoke of him again.

* * *

One night, a few weeks later, God woke me up. He told me to pick up the Bible. I flipped it open once and immediately before me was Matthew 12:43-45. The passage speaks of an unclean spirit leaving a man and seeking rest elsewhere. But when he finds none, he returns to the house he came from. When he finds it clean and set aright, he goes and returns with seven other spirits more wicked than he. They enter and live there, and the man is in a worse state than before (NKJV).

My heart raced. "What? God, what do I do?" The fear I felt was near paralyzing. Christine could not survive another ordeal.

God told me to anoint her and pray for her. As I prayed, He told me what to say. I didn't say anything to Christine when she woke up because I did not want to stir up the slightest bit of fear within her.

A week had not passed, when *Christine dreamed she was standing near a group of people. She held her head up and saw, among the group, the boy who had turned into a beast the night she burned her hand in her dream. The group seemed preoccupied, but then the boy turned his head and looked at Christine. She met his gaze directly, her gaze cold and hard. He turned to the group and whispered something. Then, they turned and walked away.*

I was flabbergasted. The boy had come back! I told Christine about the cover of protection she had received while she slept a few nights back. She was badly shaken up when I explained why she had to get that coverage. "What if they come back?" she asked, worry plastered on her face. My heart bled for her.

"I doubt they will. God made sure I knew ahead of time they were coming because He has your back like that," I said reassuringly. "However, if they do come back, you know exactly what to do. Don't you?" I watched in relief as she nodded, her face less taut.

* * *

The kids stopped going to church after they were baptized—a decision that was entirely their own. Christine and Michael stopped going first. When I asked if they were sure about their decision, Christine brought to my attention that when the angel said I had been given more time, that mercy was extended to her as well. She believed that the three rings were not just for me to nurture physically, but also spiritually. Although both boys agreed, Nathan continued to go to church because he didn't want to upset Logan. However, it became next to impossible for him to glean anything from the services because God spoke to him there: giving him instruction, revealing mysteries, giving him messages for others. Eventually, he stopped going. Nobody was happy about it, least of all Logan. And although the kids tried to convince him he was misguided, he, of course, blamed me.

My mom was equally as judgmental. She expressed reservations about my decision to leave the church to do God's bidding. In one phone call, I explained for the umpteenth time what had precipitated that move. She listened and then said, "Are you sure it's God you're hearing and not the devil? Because you know, the devil sometimes comes and whispers in our ears as well, so you have to make sure that it's really God who is talking to you."

I stewed, my blood reaching boiling point. It was all I could do to keep my voice low. "Really, Mother? Can a dog mistake someone else's voice for that of its master's? If a man has a dog that he has fed, trained, played with and loved, do you think a stranger could come along and call the dog and the dog mistake that person for his master?"

"Well . . . no . . ." she said.

Before she could say anything else, I said, "Just like a dog knows its master, I know mine. All I know is that God has called me for a special purpose. I'm just not sure what it is yet."

"Hm. God isn't going to use somebody with your disposition," my mom said snidely.

I saw red. If my mother could see my face, she would have said, "Case in point." I checked my anger and said as calmly as I could, "Mother, it's unbelievable to me that you just said that. God uses anybody He chooses regardless of who they are. Where do you get off judging me? You really don't know why God chooses who He does, and when you question Him, you're saying He doesn't know what He's doing."

My mom backed off. "You have a point. I'm just concerned for your salvation."

I wanted to say, "Don't be," but instead I said, "I know, Mommy."

At times, I wondered why I even bothered to try and make my mother understand what was happening with me spiritually because she questioned everything. However, it was extremely important to me that she understood that I had not backslidden.

One night my mom called. Christine was on my bed reading her picture Bible, so I went into another room so as not to disturb her. My mom and I spoke at length about church and kids. The conversation got heated because my mom was adamant that I allow the kids to make their own decisions regarding attending church and using devotionals. I assured her that they did; however, she sounded unconvinced still, so I told her to ask the kids herself. After I ended the call and went back into my bedroom, Christine was still there. She looked disconcerted.

"What's wrong?" I asked.

"Mom, I opened the Bible to a story God wanted me to read, and then when I was done, He gave me a message for Nana," she said, looking very worried.

I frowned. "Really? What story was it?"

"It's the story of Miriam in Numbers 12. She and Aaron spoke against Moses, and God got angry. He punished Miriam by giving her leprosy," Christine said her eyes wide. "Is God going to give Nana leprosy?"

I didn't remember the story. "What did Miriam say?"

"She said that Moses acted like he was the only one that God spoke through, so God punished her for being jealous."

I got the goosebumps. "Really? Wow. That's crazy."

Christine took up her phone. "I'm going to text her now," she said, her voice mirroring the heaviness in her heart, and I wished I could lighten her burden.

Christine was very different from me. She rarely vacillated. When God told her to do something, she did it. She had already delivered messages to several of her classmates, the school nurse and had even taken to the pulpit to give a message to the church. However, when she wrote the first message, she asked, "Do you want to see it, Mom?" She was afraid my mother would see her texts as disrespectful, and deference to one's elders is extremely important in Jamaican culture.

I shook my head and said emphatically, "No. That's between you, God and Nana. Don't be afraid to tell her whatever He tells you."

The texts Christine sent to my mother read:

> *Nana, just now, I was reading a story about Moses that God led me to in my Bible. When his sister Miriam spoke against him with their brother Aaron, God called them and spoke to them. When God finished speaking, Miriam saw that she had leprosy. Aaron begged Moses to have mercy on her, but God said that she was to be banished from the camp for seven days.*
>
> *Everything is God's will, and He has special people He calls to do His will. So, anyone who goes against the will of God—including speaking against the one God has chosen—will be punished. Anyone who seeks to override God's authority will be punished.*
>
> *Nathan, Michael and I are the three rings God has given Mom to care for under His instruction. He has*

told her what must be done with us. By speaking against what God has told her to do, you are speaking against God! You will be punished for doing so if you do not heed His warning.

When God told me that you will be punished, I prayed to Him and asked that if it is His will, He should help you. God has told me to warn you. In so doing, He is showing you mercy. Pray to Him and ask that He forgive you for speaking against His will. At the same time, ask Him to do with you what He wills.

About twenty minutes later, my mom called me extremely upset. "I just got some texts from Christine, and I don't like her tone. Was she listening to our conversation?"

I shook my head. I had hoped that, for once, my mom would have acted unpredictably. "No, I was in another room. When I came back to my bedroom, she looked scared and said she had gotten a message from God for you."

"Have you seen the texts?" she asked, really agitated.

I sighed. "No, I haven't seen them."

"Well, you should go read them. Talking about I'm jealous of you. I'm not jealous of you. I wish you nothing but the best. When you're in pain, I wish I could take your pain away. What part of me is jealous of you? And she's reprimanding me?" she said indignantly.

"You're perceiving jealousy in a way God does not intend. Do you wish me ill? No. Do you want what I have? No. But your attitude toward me regarding the things that God has told me is the problem. You do believe that I think that I'm the only one God can talk to about the kids. You've even scoffed at the fact that God would use somebody like me. However, you're also looking at the wrong person. Chrissy didn't message you. God did. Go back and look at the texts, and ask yourself if she has ever spoken to you in that manner," I said, calmly. I knew full well the tone my mom spoke of. I had been dressed down by it quite a few times, but I took no offense because I recognized it for what it was."

"Okay, Ma'am," she said, sounding deflated.

My mom was diagnosed with cholangiocarcinoma (intrahepatic bile duct cancer) a few weeks later. Everybody in the family was shocked, except my kids and me. However, we did not bring up Christine's messages to my mother. Every time she talked about her illness, she said God must be trying to tell her something. And, each time, I remained quiet, my heart tearing apart. The tumor grew aggressively, growing from two centimeters to nine centimeters in just two months. She started chemotherapy and radiation to shrink the tumor so that it could be removed.

* * *

Although Logan had filed for a divorce, he had not moved out of our house. A couple of times when I needed to go to the emergency room in the middle of the night, he drove me. When I was to have my surgery, he also drove me to the hospital. At Constance's insistence, though, a female cousin of Logan's came along to help me get dressed after the procedure. God forbid the sight of my body blind his eyes and offend his delicate sensibilities.

Before the surgery, I sat on a bench in a hallway, watching people go by. One man who did not seem to be of sound mind kept asking people for food. For the most part, I ignored him because I was seated in the second row of benches and, therefore, was nowhere near him. Logan had lent me his iPad to watch a movie while he got a nap in the car.

Quite loudly, a voice asked, "Wha mek dem chain 'im up?" (Why did they chain him?) Jamaicans often add the word "up" when describing certain actions: instead of kick: kick up, beat: beat up, slap: slap up.

I looked up to see the man not quite of sound mind looking intently at me.

"Excuse me," I said, frowning. He couldn't possibly be talking to me.

However, he continued staring at me. "Wha mek dem chain 'im up?"

"*What is he talking about?*" I wondered, looking down at the iPad to see if he was referring to something he was seeing, but the iPad was on the bench beside me, blocked entirely from view by my body.

I was totally confused. "Who?"

"Yuh husband." (Your husband.) He had tilted and jerked his head in a slight up and down motion as he said this. In Jamaica, that gesture is sometimes used to express aggression or annoyance.

My heart flip-flopped, my thoughts immediately going to the dream about the chains. It couldn't be. I frowned and asked incredulously, "What?"

As I gawked at him, he continued staring, his gaze intense, as though he were contemplating what next to say. Then, in an accusatory tone and with the same snappy jerk of his head, he asked, "Wha mek yuh nuh love yuh husband?" (Why don't you love your husband?)

I could not speak. I had suddenly become a person of interest! Quite a few people who could no longer feign disinterest openly stared, anticipating my response. Then mercifully, someone sitting close to him chimed in, distracting him. While I was relieved to be free from the man's intense glare, I was not free from the turmoil roiling within me. How did he know about the chains and the deep-seated animosity I was harboring towards my husband? I had come to expect confirmation for all the things God told me, so my shock was not so much the message, but the messenger. He wasn't even sane. Most of the other things he had said prior to and following the message, made no sense. But why was I surprised God would use such a man to confirm a prophecy? Hadn't I told my mom a few months back that God could use anyone? I was being a hypocrite.

* * *

The contact with the man of seemingly unsound mind was one I'd never forget, and it bothered me well into the weeks following my recovery. Although not all mental illnesses have ties to spiritual bondage, he had me thinking overtime about what I would do should God send me back into the church. I knew I could not repeat my past selfish mistakes. I vowed to be more vigilant and play an active role in helping to free those who were bound.

As soon as I made this vow, I came under attack. One night, *I dreamed I was at a church service. Out of the corner of my eye, I saw a figure dash behind some drapery. It stuck its head out and looked around. I immediately recognized it for what it was. Stunned, I glanced around the church. I couldn't be the only one seeing this. However, everyone was preoccupied.*

"Hey!" I shouted. "There's a demon in the church!"

The congregation just kept on singing.

I turned towards the drapes in time to see the figure dash behind a column. It was about 4 feet tall and was jet black with no distinguishable features. It did not stand or move upright, but instead, slouched its exaggeratedly gangly frame.

I looked around in disbelief. "People, there's a demon in the church!"

The singing continued as the demon dashed from place to place, hiding behind seats, columns, rostrum, drapes. He moved so fast it was hard to keep track of where he was.

I walked around, waving my hands. "Hello! You people need to listen!"

Someone got up and spoke, ushers collected the offering, and the congregation sang some more. All the while, I was yelling, unheard.

Frustrated, I grabbed a yardstick and hit the floor to show where the demon went. "He's over here!" I yelled.

The demon dashed off with me hot on its tail. I slammed the stick hard against the floor. "He's over here!"

I kept this up until I started huffing, totally exhausted.

Apparently, growing bored, the demon entered the body of a strapping worshipper, who stood at about six feet. With shoulders squared, he strutted towards the exit, pausing only to address me.

He glared at me coldly, his eyes pitch-black caverns that seemed to pierce through to my soul. I wanted to flee, but my feet were nailed to the floor. He snarled, "You see too much, and you talk too much. Coming for you."

With that, he sauntered out of the hall. Somebody raised another hymn, and the congregation belted out its sweet melody, and no one was the wiser.

Admittedly, I was a little intimidated by the threat. I calmed quickly, however, because while I had been threatened by demons in the spiritual realm many times before, no harm had actually befallen me. But things were about to get stranger still.

The following night, I was awakened by fingers clawing at my left eye. It took a few seconds for me to realize that the fingers were my own. I fought to lower my arm, but my hand was being forcibly held in place. I struggled to make sense of what was happening to me as I pushed back against the hand holding mine. It did not budge. My fingers dragged on the bottom lid of my eye, scratching the tender flesh inside and nicking the white of my eye.

I pushed against the hand but to no avail. My body felt weighted, and my brain vibrated. Recognizing the force I was fighting against, I said, "I rebuke you in the name of Jesus Christ of Nazareth!"

Still, my fingers were being pressed against my eye. I struggled and rebuked for what seemed like forever, but the force of the hold did not lessen. I was frustrated and weary. I finally said, "You have no authority over me and therefore cannot harm me. I command you to release me in the name of Jesus Christ of Nazareth!"

Immediately, my hand was released, and the demon left, his license to oppress this Believer revoked.

Legion

During a period of greater than usual financial challenges, I approached God with my concerns one day. "How am I going to manage?" I asked in despair.

Immediately, He responded, "You will never be hungry, and you will never beg for bread."

I sighed my relief. "Thank you, God."

A couple days later when I told Logan what God had said to me, he gave me a weird look and asked skeptically, "Really?"

That response really put my back up. "Yes," I replied a little too firmly.

He snickered and said scornfully, "That's good for you. As for me, I have no such assurance."

I could have kicked myself for bothering, but I had hoped to, by some miracle, get a different than usual response.

It was so easy to believe in God's promises when things were going well. However, whenever the weeds of doubt threatened to choke the seeds of hope God planted in me, He would step in and remind me of His promise. He often used the children of Israel and how He provided for their needs daily, without fail, to reassure me of His faithfulness. The children of Israel were told how much manna to gather each day for each person in their household. Some gathered much, and some gathered little. However, when the manna was weighed, the ones who had gathered much did not have too much, and the ones who had gathered little did not have too little. Everyone had gathered just what they needed (Exodus 16:17-18, NIV). And it was enough.

To further reassure me, God messaged me in a dream one night. *I was about to prepare something for my family to eat but only found the end portion of a loaf of bread on the kitchen counter. I began searching desperately for the rest of the bread because that small piece of bread was not enough to share for everybody. I looked everywhere, and finally found the larger portion of the bread hidden in the back of a cupboard.*

Exasperated, I held it out to my husband and asked, "What's this? Why did you hide the bread?"

I picked up the small piece of bread in my other hand and held it for him to see. "Look. This small piece that you left out is not enough to share for all of us."

"You can't use that bread," he said firmly.

I exploded. "Why not?"

"Because it's reserved for other people." He was matter-of-fact and relatively calm.

I gasped, "But this isn't enough!" I waved the small piece of bread near his face for good measure, just in case his eyesight was defective.

He was unmoved. "Put the bread back, and leave it alone. Don't use it."

I put the bread back and walked away, angry and distressed.

"God, what am I going to do? We don't have enough to eat," I cried out.

"Prepare the portion of bread that you have," God said.

I cut the bread into small cubes, and every member of my family was fed. When we were done eating, I gathered a platterful of left-overs.

When I awoke, I lay still for a while, meditating on what God had done for my family and me in the dream. In response to my amazement, He said, "I take care of the birds, so why wouldn't I take care of you?"

I had read Matthew 6:25-34 (NIV) a few times before, but because

God brought it up, I knew it was important to read it again. Jesus admonished in this passage that worry accomplishes nothing and encouraged me to have faith that God will always provide for my needs. Just as He knows what the birds need, He knows what I need. Instead of being desirous of material things, though, I need to seek the Kingdom of God first and foremost, and in so doing, I will have all that I need. God promised me in that dream that whatever little I have, He will multiply. And it will always be enough.

* * *

As a day did not go by wherein I was tested, God said to me a few weeks later, "I want you to give Sister Daisy some money."

"Ok, God. How much?" I asked.

The amount He told me was about three-quarters of all I had left for the rest of the month. Stunned I thought, *What? But if I do that, I won't be able to pay my bills. How am I going to manage?"* I began hyperventilating but then chided myself, *"Nothing I have belongs to me, so I have to give it away if God says give it away."*

I said, "Ok God. I'll do as you ask." Funny that I do this all the time, think first and then speak to God, often forgetting that He hears my every thought.

That Sunday, I arranged for my nephew Justin to pass a message to Sister Daisy while I sat in my car outside the church gate. She came out, face beaming. "Sister Jabez! I'm so happy to see you. I ask for you all the while," she said, hugging me tightly.

I didn't flinch. Instead, I melted into the warmth of her embrace. "It's nice to see you too, Sister Daisy. It's been a long time," I said, grinning.

I stepped back and held on firmly to both her arms. "Sister Daisy, don't think it strange, but God sent me to give you something." I pulled the envelope from my pocket and handed it to her.

"How can I think it strange, Sister Jaye? I'll never forget the night I saw the angel standing beside you in the church. I knew for sure, then, that you belong to God. I don't care what anybody else says about you because you're not coming to church."

I smiled. "God also said to tell you that He has not forgotten you," I said, delivering the message I got on my drive over to the church.

Sister Daisy gasped, her eyes welling up. "You have no idea how much that means to me. Sister Jaye, I've been having so many problems in my family, and I've been feeling so stressed out and alone." She paused and looked up to heaven. "Oh God," she cried passionately. "Thank you. Thank you." She looked back at me. "Sister Jaye, please pray for my family."

I nodded, glancing nervously towards the church. I really didn't want anyone to see me there. I quickly hugged her. "I will," I promised, climbing into my car. "Oh, one more thing . . . don't tell anyone about this." I hadn't planned on saying that, and I'm not at all sure why I did.

The next morning, Abigail called me. "Hey, I have your pay. God said to give it to you today."

I gasped. "But it's the middle of the month."

"I know, but it's what God says."

I laughed, "You're not going to believe this . . ."

* * *

Sometime later, *I dreamed that Emma and I were at the hospital waiting for my mother to come out of surgery. After a long while, a doctor with a warm smile and twinkly eyes came out and said, "Everything is okay. The surgery was a success. Your mother will be in recovery about two hours, and then you can see her."*

I sighed in relief. Two hours was a long time to wait, so Emma and I decided to go home. We showered and got something to eat. When we got back to the hospital, the surgeon we had spoken to earlier came over, except this time, his countenance was markedly different. He was aloof, his eyes not quite meeting either of ours.

"I'm sorry, but there was a complication. Your mother started bleeding internally. We worked assiduously to stop the bleeding, but then, one by one her organs began shutting down. There was nothing we could do. I'm sorry," he said solemnly.

"Nooooo," I screamed, my hands resting on my head. "You said everything was okay. That's what you said. How could things go so horribly wrong in such a short time?"

"We did everything we could. I'm sorry for your loss," he said before walking away.

My sister and I hugged each other tightly and wept bitterly.

When I woke up, I was filled with dread. My mother was going to die. I toyed with the idea of telling her but decided against it. Instead of being preoccupied with the fear of dying, I wanted her to focus on the hope of surviving.

A few days later, she called sounding a bit frazzled. "Did you dream anything?"

My eyes widened. "Why?"

"Nothing," she said way too softly, sounding like she was far away. "I'm just asking because I can't shake this funny feeling."

I paused a few seconds too long, and then I lied to my mother. "No, I got nothing. No dreams. No feeling. Nothing."

"Okay. Good," she said, sighing in relief.

I didn't feel good when I hung up from her, and I could only go to one place with that. "God, I'm sorry. I couldn't tell her the truth. I really couldn't," I cried, my heart bleeding profusely. "Please, please show her mercy. She doesn't get it. I don't know if she'll ever get it, but I'm begging you to give her a chance. Please."

Silence. I waited. Still nothing. I eventually gave up. I would ask again tomorrow.

A few weeks later, my mom called with the surgery date. September 10. Seriously? Without knowing it, she had just told me when she was going to die. My belly bottom was being adversely affected by gravity. "God, please. Michael's birthday? And just one day before Mommy's birthday? Really? I am begging you to show Mommy mercy, please," I pleaded, tears pooling, stinging the corners of my eyes.

Silence. I waited. Still nothing. I eventually gave up. I would ask again tomorrow. The tears I had been fighting hard to keep in check fell freely.

Several days later, I turned on my T.V. Hurricane Irma was heading to Florida. It was slated to make landfall a couple days before my mother's surgery. My heart leaped. Maybe the doctors would reschedule. If they did, then I knew she would be okay. I waited impatiently by the phone for news. My mom eventually called to say the surgery was postponed for a week. As I hung up, I grinned, looked up to Heaven and mouthed, "Thank you."

* * *

On Grand Market, the night before Christmas, two kinds of people, the meanderers and the revelers, usually thronged the streets until the wee hours of the morning. Quite a noisy affair: music, food, alcohol, firecrackers, window shoppers, last-minute shoppers, idlers. I never enjoyed Grand Market as a child, so I never took the kids. Instead, we baked cookies and watched Hallmark movies until four in the morning while we waited up for Logan. In our town, Logan's family's business was one of the lead places to gift shop. I never got into the spirit of

Christmas. I agreed with the Grinch, before he, unfortunately, had a change of heart, that there was nothing to love about Christmas.

One year when the kids were very young, I tried convincing them that Christmas trees were just hype. I'd catch the funny glances they threw in each other's direction every time I gave my "trees are overrated" speech. They apparently weren't buying what I was selling, and I wasn't buying a tree. So as a compromise, I draped an oversized umbrella with tinsel and some lights. I even hung a huge bauble off the pointy top. I was very pleased with myself and hoped the kids were impressed with my ingenuity. I promised with a hundred and ten percent surety that no one else in the world had a tree like theirs. My kids were great and never once complained to my face. And then, Christine went to school and wrote about it, with illustrations to boot. I felt a little sheepish when her teacher showed me the paper and told me that she had given Christine an "A" for creativity. Then, because I was never adept at playing poker, she took one look at my face and exclaimed in disgust, "This is true?" Well . . . I never did that again.

* * *

The holidays were now fast approaching, and celebrating with a divorce looming did nothing to improve my usual sour Christmastime disposition. The only thing worth celebrating was my mother's successful surgery. The doctors had removed her gall bladder and half of her liver, and she was recovering nicely. She was cheery and chatty, and it was great to pick up the phone whenever I wanted to and hear her voice.

On the day after Christmas, a public holiday called Boxing Day, lots of people hang out with friends and extended family or go on outings. I always preferred staying in bed and watching a good movie. I really was not in the mood to have anybody over, but Logan decided he wanted to have a get-together. When I asked him who was coming, he was evasive. That I did not like. I could deal with his family, but I was not up to entertaining any of his friends, especially Lowell. I called Abigail a few days before Boxing Day to complain that I couldn't manage the cooking and could not afford to feed that many people.

Abigail said calmly, "What are you worried about? You have food."

"I do?" I asked, surprised.

"Yes. I have food, so you have food," she said, quite matter-of-fact.

George and Abigail threw big shindigs at their home every Boxing Day, and I had been about four times. Every year, they had as many as three hundred guests pass through.

Boxing Day morning, as the kids and I ate breakfast, God said, "Anoint the children."

I did not think twice. I just did it. Then, as I was about to put away the olive oil, He said, "Anoint yourself."

"What?" I asked, quite shocked. "People don't anoint themselves." In the church I had gone to when I was young, I learned that the elders were the ones who did the anointing. "This is kind of weird," I admitted. "But I'll do it because You said so."

All I prepared for dinner that day was potato salad and mac and cheese. Whatever Abigail had not dropped off on Grand Market night, Logan picked up on Boxing Day. I had a lavish spread of mannish water (soup made with goat head and tripe), roast beef, roast pork, roast fish, curried goat, ham, jerked chicken, jerked pork, baked chicken, lobster and a variety of sides, juices and desserts, including sorrel, a traditional Jamaican Christmas drink and Jamaican fruit cake, a black cake with blended fruits and rum.

As I watched the first guests arrive, my heart sank. It was extremely awkward greeting Lowell and his family. He was cold, and his wife was lukewarm at best. When I went to hug one of their daughters, she drew back with dramatic flair, looking me up and down with disdain. It was going to be a long day. The party was made up extensively of Logan's friends. However, I had invited one of my cousins and his wife. He was the one whose house I had considered running away to when I was seven. He was fantastic company, and it didn't hurt that he was a chef. The lobster had to be cooked fresh, and I had no clue what I was doing. My interaction with the guests was most uncomfortable. However, I sucked it all up and was the perfect hostess. I waited on the guests, hand and foot.

A couple days later, while I was lamenting the nerve of Logan to invite people into our home who openly held me in disdain, Nathan knocked on my door. He looked ready to burst he was so excited. "Mom, God said that He prepared a table before you in the presence of your enemies."

"Huh?" I said, confused.

"Boxing Day," Nathan said.

My face lit up. "Seriously?"

"Yes, and not only that. He also said He anointed your head with oil."

I grinned. "Really? Do you know what's cool? I was just feeling sorry for myself."

"You were?" he asked, raising his eyebrows. "I was wondering why God told me to tell you that." He smiled. "Well, there you go. You were well prepared."

I chuckled. "Yeah, I was."

* * *

One day, a couple months later, God said, "Call forth a legion of angels."

I was shocked and somewhat perturbed. Why did I need to summon angels? And why so many? How could I tell this to anybody at all? This bordered on extremely bizarre; however, it was what God commanded. So, I raised my hand towards Heaven and summoned a legion of angels, admittedly feeling somewhat silly. I didn't question God at all. A legion was plenty, and that meant I probably didn't want to know. I tried convincing myself not to be too concerned about whether the legion of angels had actually come. After all, how was I going to know? Curious cat that I was, though, I couldn't feign nonchalance. I thought about it often and the not knowing was eating me.

About two weeks later, a Believer, who had given me several messages from God, said to me, "Teacher, I got a vision of you, and you were surrounded by angels."

My hand flew to my mouth. "What? Really?" I barely managed to choke out. My heart drummed an irregular rhythm. It was a good thing I was sitting. Although I had grown accustomed to her visions of my family and her messages for me, this was by far the one that floored me most.

Her face exuded sheer wonder. "Yes, teacher, it was a whole heap o' angels," she said sweeping her hand over the expanse of the large room to indicate that they were many.

"What? Seriously?" I asked really goosebumpy, my thoughts racing. This was beyond surreal.

"Yes, teacher," she said, stressing her words. "They were different sizes . . . some very big . . . some pretty small," she said, using her hands to indicate height and girth. "They were all dressed in long, white flowy gowns.

My breath caught in my throat. When I could speak, "Oh my God," was all I could manage to say.

"Teacher, I never imagined so many angels could be around one person," she said. I could tell from the far-away look on her face that she was envisioning her vision.

"What were they doing?" I asked, eager to know. Maybe that would give a clue as to why God had told me to call them.

"Not much of anything." She moved her arm in a slow, circular motion and said, "They were just all around you." She continued chatting excitedly, but I was hearing her in a fog.

"They did come," I thought dreamily.

All Things Being Equal

Right after the holidays, Emma called to tell me that our mom was in the hospital. She had ascites (abnormal build-up of fluid in her abdominal cavity), a blood clot in her left leg and edema (fluid retention) in her feet, ankles, and legs. She had been improving steadily and was back to doing some of the things she loved. So, what happened? Since Emma had gone to Florida for my mom's surgery and had recently made a trip to help care for her, we decided I would go.

My mom was in pretty bad shape. Apparently, her complications were caused by an adverse reaction to her radiation treatment. She had to spend about three weeks in the hospital. When she returned home, she had to receive round-the-clock care. My hyper-organized younger sister assisted me for about a week, which was a lifesaver. She set timers on my cell phone for my mom's meds—I still wrote everything down on paper—bought tubs to pool supplies, filed doctors' names and contact information, and logged every upcoming appointment.

My mom had difficulty walking and was in constant pain. Her blood pressure was very low and had to be monitored. Although she had an excellent nurse, who came twice a day, I had to do the monitoring in between. She was throwing up and had to have pureed foods. Twice a week, she had to get a paracentesis, a procedure in which a needle was used to extract excess fluids from her abdomen. My dad and one of my mom's sisters drove us to those appointments. As the days went by, my mom's tall, slender stature grew more and more Weeble-esque. The first time I tidied her, I recoiled when I took her blouse off. Her back, shoulders, and arms were skin and bones. Every bone of her collar, shoulder, chest and rib cage was clearly distinguishable, a stark contrast to what was going on from her midriff down.

I hardly slept at night. I grew more and more exhausted with each passing day until I started feeling unwell. Stress caused my lupus to flare. I was finding it hard to care for myself much less tend to my mom's needs, so I decided to hand off my mom's care to Emma. Two days before I left, I prayed for my mom, gently resting my hand on her shoulder. I did not ask for her to be healed but for God's will to be done.

Emma called me a couple days after she arrived in Florida. "Why did you tell me to come? Mommy doesn't need me. You made it sound like she was in very bad shape."

That got my back up. "What do you mean? I kept you posted regarding all that was going on. You know how hard it was for me. I am beyond exhausted because I had to take care of Mommy round-the-clock." I was offended that she made it sound as though I had exaggerated our mom's condition. But I kept my calm. "Well, the day before I left, she said she didn't want her food pureed. Instead, she wanted me to mash her potatoes and pumpkin. And she did ask for seconds, which surprised me. I don't get it though, what do you mean when you say she doesn't need you?"

"Well, for one, she's walking around unassisted, the swelling in her abdomen has gone down, so her next scheduled paracentesis was canceled, she's eating solid foods—salmon, mashed potatoes, bagels—she's not throwing up, and she even came into the kitchen to show me how to use her toaster oven."

My mouth fell open. I did not understand what was going on. Emma was describing a totally different woman than the one I had left there. In just a few days, my mom had apparently improved drastically. Every time we had asked the doctors for a prognosis, their expressions turned glum. One of my mom's neighbors whose wife died of cancer told me that she had started retaining water in the end. Many prayer requests went out for my mom, and I knew God answered prayers, but I had a feeling that there was something I was missing. It wasn't until a few days after the conversation with my sister that I got a message from God to count the number of weeks between when my mom had gone into the hospital and when she started to take a dramatic turn for the better. It had been seven weeks! I was totally freaked out by this because Miriam could not return to camp for seven days. This was beyond incredible to me. I would have loved to discuss this revelation and its implications with my mom, but in light of her reaction to Christine's warning, I decided it was best to just let it rest.

* * *

My eyes flew open. I looked around the dark room, trying to get my bearings. Where was I? I vaguely made out the shape of a desk. I was at my mom's house. The only discernible sound in the still of the early morning was my heart hammering against my chest. My lungs were starved for oxygen, and I struggled to intake air. I had just witnessed something unspeakably horrific, except I couldn't remember what it was. I fought to recall what I had seen, but the only thing that came to mind was a date: July 16, 2018. I began hyperventilating. I vaguely remembered seeing an angel. Had he shown me something? Maybe he had simply told it to me. I couldn't remember which. I told myself that if it was important, I would remember when the time was right. Because there was no use losing sleep over something I couldn't remember, I tried lulling myself to sleep by listening to Donnie McClurkin's "Speak to my Heart." However, that did not work, as all I could hear in my head was, "July 16, 2018. July 16, 2018 . . ."

I gave up, flicked the switch, grabbed the nearest piece of paper and wrote: *July 16, 2018 (Got this date in a dream: 5/27/18)*

After a long while, I fell into a fitful sleep.

Not remembering scared me, and that uncertainty fed my fear. What did it mean that I had gotten a date? The feeling of dread was so overpowering that I had to get it under control before it consumed me. I talked myself down from the ledge by focusing on the sensory—what was "real." As the days sped by uneventfully, I calmed.

* * *

About a month later, *I dreamed that I was inside a house, watching two boys play on a circular rug. One of the boys was me. I sensed a sinister presence upstairs. I leaned over and whispered to my brother, "He's upstairs."*

We ran past me up the stairs and burst into a room. The room was huge and had walls made of slats of wood laid horizontally. The wood was gray and hollow-looking, as if in an advanced state of decay, with tons of cracks that had stripped away the wood in places, leaving noticeable splinters. The floor fared no better. In the middle of the otherwise empty room was a huge clock. The face of the clock contained events instead of numbers, and the devil was controlling each event. Each time the minute hand moved, a disaster took place somewhere in the world.

Tick . . . tick . . . tick . . . tick . . . tick . . .

"Stop!" I screamed.

But the devil ignored me, focused on what he was doing. Desperate, I looked around the room, and that's when I noticed his arsenal. How had we not seen the weapons before? He didn't have to go anywhere to wield any of them. A weapon would disappear at the instance an event was to take place. I watched in horror.

My brother and I shouted over and over again for the devil to stop, but he ignored us. "You're killing thousands and thousands of people," I cried, trying to appeal to his sense of . . . not sure what. When my plea fell on deaf ears, I tried to grab a hold of him, but I could not touch him.

Defeated, my brother and I went back downstairs. "The only way we're going to stop him is to trick him. We have to get him out of the house," I said.

We huddled close and devised a plan. We loathed a face-to-face with the devil, so we remained downstairs.

"Your plan's failing," my brother shouted up to him.

"That's right," I yelled. "As we speak, there are angels at all the locations you targeted. They are helping people and foiling the attacks you set in motion."

I felt him leave with a whoosh and the heaviness lift. We raced upstairs, not sure how much time we would have. We had to hurry. We grabbed all the weapons, which were not like any weapons that could be described. It was more like each article was symbolic of something ominous. We ran for what seemed like miles, careful not to be followed, and found a place to hide the weapons. We cloaked them with a powerful shield of prayer and left satisfied that it would be a long while before the devil could get his hands on them again.

Huffing and puffing, we hurried home. Just as we settled back on the floor and were catching our breaths, I felt the abysmal force return. I leaned over and whispered, "He's back."

My brother gasped, looking distressed. "Already? What are we going to do?"

"Come on." I grabbed his hand, and we stealthily made our way upstairs. I wasn't sure what we would do once we got there, but I knew we could not not do anything.

As we entered the room, we both gasped. We didn't even spare the devil a second glance, our focus solely on the clock. The hands of the clock were spinning extremely fast. As we watched in horror, disaster after disaster took place in rapid succession.

Tickticktickticktick . . .

We had stopped nothing. We had, in fact, made things worse.

"No," I whispered, backing away slowly and shaking my head vigorously. "What have we done?"

I spoke so softly, I almost didn't hear me. I looked from the clock to my face, from my face to the clock, feeling myriad emotions because my anguish was palpable.

I startled from my sleep, not sure at all what the dream meant. I knew it had to do with end times, which would account for the horrible events that the devil was manipulating. I had had many similar dreams, which all ended the same . . . with death and destruction. Nothing could be done in any of those dreams to pre-empt the catastrophes that are slated to happen in the last days. Maybe it was a cautionary message not to focus on what I was powerless to change, but instead, focus on what I needed to change. Whatever it meant, time was running out.

When God "messages me" in dreams and I am unclear, I sometimes ask for clarification while I'm in a dream, but if I don't get that opportunity, I ask once I'm awake. I have never asked a question for which I have not received an answer, even if the answer is simply that I don't need to know. I didn't ask about this dream, however, because as disconcerting as it was, its abstractness did not evoke as much angst as the specific date, July 16, which was steadily approaching.

* * *

On July 15, as I lay in bed struggling to fall asleep, unable to forget the impending date, God asked me, "When are you going to forgive your father?" I was happy to hear Him speak. It had been a few weeks, and I was missing our conversations. I didn't, however, like the subject matter.

"Soon," I said, hoping that that would be the end of that particular line of questioning.

"What are you waiting for?" He asked.

I sighed. "I'm waiting for Emma."

It made perfect sense for us to talk to my father together because deep down, I hoped that she would do most of the talking. One bird, two stones. Quick and easy. Clever me.

The amusement was mine alone, however. "You are responsible for your own salvation," God admonished fearsomely. And then, He was gone, leaving me well and truly chastised.

I was in trouble. I had intentionally postponed talking to my father many times, always with the promise that I'd do it tomorrow. However, I could tell that this time was different. I was bummed. I needed to talk to my father immediately. Problem was, it was late, and my father was already in bed. As I closed my eyes, I promised, "Okay, God, I promise I'll do it tomorrow."

The next morning, I got side-tracked with mundane tasks: breakfast, bills, phone calls, laundry. By the time I eventually thought to talk to my father, he announced he was going on the road. The day was sunny and fair when my father headed out the door. Not five minutes later, a deafening, high-pitched, crackling noise danced across the sky, followed by an explosion so loud I almost jumped out of my skin. Immediately, an image of my father lying dead underneath the ackee tree (Jamaican national fruit tree) flashed into my mind. I instantly dismissed it and continued doing what I was doing because my father was long gone. Then, a key turned in the front door, and my father came in looking extremely shaken.

Startled, I said "You're still here? I thought you had left."

His voice trembling, my dad said, "Just as I was about to leave, I got a phone call, so I went under the ackee tree to talk. All of a sudden, I heard a loud boom, and the leaves above my head shook really hard." He raised both hands and shook his fists violently to demonstrate just how hard. "The day looked so clear, the last thing I expected was lightning. That was close." He shuddered and fell quiet as if lost in thought.

I pulled the blinds and looked outside. The sky was crystal clear and blue. My mom, who had been listening keenly to the account, slowly turned her head and met my gaze. "What date is it today?" she asked, her voice a combination of excitement and fear.

Oh boy, cue the *Twilight Zone* theme song. I just stared at her, not wanting to journey where she was trying to take me.

Not deterred, she asked, "Isn't it the sixteenth?"

I nodded.

My dad looked lost. "What is it about the sixteenth?" he asked.

I couldn't speak. I got up and retrieved the index card I had written the date on and held it up to him, hoping it was self-explanatory. But my father just stared blankly at it, so I filled him in. I could not be sure how much of it actually registered, however, because he said nothing once I had finished. As I watched him sipping a cup of tea to steady his nerves, I thought, equally shaken, *"Wow, Daddy was supposed to die. That was what was too horrible to remember."*

I shuddered. I needed to talk to God about the opportunity I had lost and beg Him for a second chance. I quietly slipped away to be alone with him. "Oh God, please forgive me and show me mercy. Please, please, please give me a second chance." I begged, my eyes welling with tears.

"I will show you mercy," God said, and I let out a huge sigh of relief. But then, He added, "Only because Jesus has interceded on your behalf."

I inhaled sharply, and my pulse quickened. Hearing the reason God was showing me mercy stunned me. How many times had I heard or read in Romans 8:34 that Jesus was seated at God's right hand interceding for us? However, I never imagined an instant when Jesus would actually be speaking up for me. This was extraordinarily unbelievable. I thanked God for being merciful, and then I turned my attention to Jesus, calling Him by every name I could remember, including, Friend.

As I sat across from my father that night, a bundle of nerves and raw emotions, I struggled to get out what I wanted to say. However, my father was very helpful. "Name one time I hit you because I don't remember ever hitting you. I can remember hitting each of your sisters once."

I saw stars. "I don't need to do that, and I don't want to do that. What's the use?" I had raised my voice just a little.

"I don't remember. Remind me," he coaxed.

After I recounted the details of one incident, my father asked in disbelief, "I beat you for that?"

"Yes, you did," I said defensively. Did he think I was making it up?

"Why would I do that?" he asked.

I gasped and asked incredulously, "How should I know?"

"Why didn't you explain? I'm sure I would have understood," my father chided.

That got my back up, and I retorted, "No, you wouldn't have. You beat first and asked questions later . . . no wait . . . that was Mommy. You just beat."

"So, who beat you more? Me or Mommy?" he asked, and before I could reply, he rocked back in his seat and said quite smugly, "I bet it was Mommy because she was with you guys more."

My mouth gaped open. "What does it matter? Maybe she did, maybe she didn't, but she apologized a long time ago." That wiped the smug off his face. "Plus, we're not talking about her. We're talking about you." My father had the uncanny ability to make anything and everything my mother's fault, and I resented that.

My father's expression grew somber as he said, "I don't know if I told you about my childhood—"

"Yes, you did, several times. And while I feel bad for you, which I've told you before, none of what you endured excuses your behavior.

I don't beat and intimidate my kids because I made a conscious decision to break the cycle of abuse."

My father looked startled. "You think you were abused?"

"Of course," I cried.

My father was totally oblivious. It was that disconnect which accounted for what my father did next. He pointed to the more than half-century-year-old scars on his body, artfully resuscitating each one with an abysmal tale painstakingly spun. I listened, disappointed by his response. *"This is impossible. I cannot forgive this man,"* I thought.

"Why not," God asked.

"Because he's making this about him," I said angrily. "He hasn't even said he's sorry."

"He does not have to be sorry," God said.

"Why not?" I asked in disbelief.

"Your forgiving your father has never been about him, it has always been about you. It has been about you doing what is hardest for you to do—let go."

As I stared wordlessly at my father, he suddenly stopped talking and studied me intently. "So, what am I to take away from this conversation?" he asked. I said nothing. "Am I to take it that I am forgiven?"

I hesitated momentarily, averting my eyes. One of my sisters had a damaged back. One had scars that never quite faded despite my mother's warm water and Epsom salt ministrations. And me? I had a damaged jaw, my TMJ so bad that I used to sometimes yawn, and my jaw would lock in the open position. What about the emotional scars? Those that changed forever the person I could have been. I thought about the baggage on top of the bus. My baggage served me well over the years, keeping me: sad, angry, lonely, frustrated, jaded, cynical, distrustful, wary. I didn't realize, until that moment, how physically tired I was. Unforgiveness was exhausting. The desperation that I felt for my father to understand and regret the damage inflicted, melted away. I locked eyes with his and said softly, "Yes."

* * *

One day, God asked me how many weeks there were between when I had the July 16 dream and the actual date. I was bewildered. What did it matter? I counted anyway—because well, God asked—and got seven weeks. I was totally freaked out. First, it took seven weeks for my mom to get better, and now this? Had I remembered my dream and warned my father he was to die in seven weeks, what would he have done with his time? I had seven weeks in which to forgive him and did absolutely nothing with that time. In all the years I have been getting dreams and having visions, I never once got a date. Why had I gotten a date for my parents? One thing is sure, God does not discriminate. Even though the nature of my relationship is different with each of my parents, they both got the same time.

* * *

I had to go to Maryland to be with Emma because she needed to have emergency surgery. She had multiple tumors that couldn't be biopsied but presented as cancer in so many ways, her oncologist was about ninety percent sure she had cancer.

I kept Emma's company while she was being prepped for surgery, not too thrilled she chose an inopportune time such as that to remind me about her life insurance policies and other benefits, just in case. When it was time for me to retire to the waiting area, I was worried, but I did not let on. As I looked back at her and waved, I thought "*I hope the cancer hasn't spread.*"

After I had watched over four agonizing hours of courtroom dramas—who knew there were so many—Emma's surgeon put me out of my misery. The preliminary pathology report showed that Emma did not have cancer. My shoulders sagged as I let out a huge sigh of relief. I stayed with Emma for two weeks before returning to Florida.

It was then my mom started waking up the entire house, yelling, shrieking and fighting in her sleep. The sounds she made were loud, ugly and desperate and made the hairs on my neck back stand up. Every time I asked about the dreams, she said there was a man trying to get in through the front door. I simply chalked it up to a side effect of chemotherapy.

* * *

Then one night, *I dreamed that I frantically ran to the front door because there was something menacing coming. The huge, black, billowy entity and I reached the door simultaneously. I braced my hands against the door, pushing outward just as the shadowy mass tried to push the door in. The energy radiating from the mass created a powerful, ominous force that threatened to push me back. I had seen an entity like this in a dream once before, many years ago, except it wasn't as large. It shadowed my mother-in-law, and they moved in tandem with each other like partners in a dance. I braced hard against the door, groaning and grunting as I struggled to keep it from being pushed in. I heard God's voice, and I repeated everything He told me to say. Suddenly, a pure, white light radiated from beneath my hands. I was emitting a colossal amount of energy that was as powerful as the energy on the other side of the door. The forces on both sides of the door were now equal, and I was able to hold the door.*

Before Journey's End

Nathan and I waited, on edge, as the doctor tore open the large white envelope containing Nathan's test results. As she read the report to herself, her face gave away nothing: no frown, raised eyebrows, change in breathing. I guess she was more adept at playing poker than I was. She perused the multi-page document several times before telling us that Nathan had a growth on his thyroid gland that would need to be biopsied. I was mortified. First my mom, then Emma and now Nathan. I could not afford to fall apart, though, because I had to do a convincing job of assuring Nathan that he would be fine.

A week later, I got an urging to pick up a game I was not in the mood to play. After about ten minutes of resisting, I gave in. I had over twenty word games that I was playing with friends. I tapped open a random board, and there on the screen, in neon pink, was the word BIOPSY that I had played two weeks before.

My mouth fell open. "God, what's this? You've never shown me anything in this way before." I marveled as I stared at the word BIOPSY, boxed in by other words that had since been built around it. However, I quickly checked myself. I was being silly . . . reading too much into something that was probably mere happenstance.

Then God said, "You are to pray for Nathan, but only after the biopsy." Okaaay . . . not a coincidence.

"That's really bizarre," I thought. I wanted to ask why it mattered when I prayed for my son. But then, because God always has a reason, I said instead, "Okay, God. I'll do what You say."

247

I had to tell somebody about this, so I immediately called Emma. As I spoke, God brought Christine to mind and how she had been healed after I laid hands on her. I didn't say anything to Emma because as far as I was concerned, what happened with Christine was a one-off occurrence. Instead, I rambled on about the message in the game. Then, God spoke.

"Emma, God just said that I prayed for Mommy. I did pray for her . . . but I didn't even pray for her to be healed. I just prayed that God's will be done . . . and that was only once . . . and I didn't touch her head like I did Christine's. I only touched her shoulder . . . Oh my God!"

"Wha' happen?" Emma asked, startled at my outburst.

"I touched her! What is God saying? Is He saying that my prayer healed her? But Mommy said she went to a prayer meeting, and a Bahamian man prayed for her. When he touched her, a warm feeling flowed through her, so when she started getting better, I thought it was that prayer that had healed her. Besides, the man said that he has never prayed for anybody that didn't get healed."

"I never believed he healed her. Remember that after he prayed for her, she still continued to get worse? How is that?"

"Well, maybe it just took some time. Maybe it was a process."

"Oh," Emma said, but it wasn't an "oh, I see," oh. It was more like an "oh, I don't know about that," oh.

Then I paused to listen to hear what God was saying. "Oh my God. God just said that when someone is healed, they are immediately healed."

"Wow, that's amazing, and it makes perfect sense. Look at when Mommy started getting better."

"Yes, it does make sense. When Jesus prayed for the lame man, the man immediately took up his bed and walked. He didn't lay there for two days or a week. When the woman with the issue of blood touched his garment, her bleeding immediately stopped. Oh my God!" I stopped in the middle of my rambling to listen to God. "God just said I prayed for you. I don't remember that. Did I pray for you?"

"I don't remember that." Emma paused to think a little before she said, "No."

My heart sank. I know what I just heard, and I know that I didn't hear wrong. "Are you sure? Maybe I prayed for you at your apartment."

"No, I don't think so," Emma said, her tone sounding doubtful.

Then, God spoke. "God says that when you asked me to pray for you, you said it's because He hears me more."

"Oh, yes," Emma cried. "I remember saying that! It was just before they came to take me to the operating room."

"I remember now," I said thinking hard. However, the details were still unclear. "Did I touch you? Maybe on your head . . . no . . . I don't remember touching your head."

"You didn't touch me." Her voice held a note of something I couldn't quite put a finger on.

"Are you sure?" I could not let it go. "Think hard. Did I put my hand on you any at all?"

"Actually, we held hands."

I gasped as goose bumps tickled my skin, and my head seemed to grow a little. "Oh my God. That's it. That is why the doctors didn't find any sign of cancer."

"Jabez, this is incredible. All of this is unbelievable!"

My heart sped up a little. "You're telling me. First Chrissy, then Mommy, then you. I would never be so presumptuous as to think that God would use me to heal anybody besides Christine. I just didn't make the connection at all, and I never would if God had not spelled it out for me. This is crazy. I think the gift of healing is just so out there . . . so special. I'd watch people being healed on T.V. and be in awe of it."

Emma chuckled. "Yeah, I know. I, for one, am happy that you have it."

When I got off the phone, I had mixed feelings: wonderment, happiness, excitement, apprehension, fear. If all of this was true, I wanted to pray for Nathan right away to stem his suffering. But then, I remembered the morning I woke up from the dream in which I had to hold the door against the menacing force trying to get to my mother. God had said to me, "Anoint the front door."

When my mom saw me anoint the door, she asked me to anoint the other doors and the windows as well. "I can't," I said, indignantly. "God did not tell me to do that."

I had to take that stance in all things because it is not I who saves. And so, when God said wait to pray for Nathan, hard as it was, I waited.

***

I got invited to church by a close friend of fourteen years, and because I had decided I would no longer hide from the people who mattered to me, I told her the truth instead of simply making up an excuse as to why I could not go. She admitted she would need time to process some of the things I was telling her but assured me she didn't think me weird. She expressly stated that she did not agree with my leaving the church because the Bible says not to forsake the assembling of ourselves together. To solidify her point, she said, "God is not going to tell you to do something that contradicts the Bible."

At this, I mentioned Abraham and how he was asked to do something that was contrary, something God had never asked of anyone before and has not asked of anyone since. I explained that my situation was similar. When she asked what my purpose was, I gave her a list. Unconvinced still, she asked, "But what is your ultimate purpose?"

That perplexed me. I floundered, not sure at all what to say. I had never felt so unsure since the start of my journey. When I hung up, she didn't have an answer, and I was near tears. I went to the only place I could go. "Why?" I cried out bitterly. "She's just like everyone else. Other people are going to have the same issues and the same questions. I couldn't even handle myself properly. I tripped all over myself and didn't even say half the things I should have said. Ultimate purpose? Whoever heard of an ultimate purpose? Please help me understand exactly what I'm doing."

"You are living the Bible," God said.

That floored me. "What?" I was a bit taken aback, but then I thought about all the things that had happened to me over the years, and it made sense. I had often wondered about the bizarre nature of some of my experiences, but I never tied them to the Bible in that way. Sure, I saw some parallels, but never would I have put it like that. I grinned. "Actually, that's pretty crazy-cool, and it explains a lot."

"What are the color of the rings?" God then asked.

I was caught off guard, "Huh?"

"What are the color of the rings?

"I don't remember," I said, confused. Why was God bringing up the color of the rings after all this time? I tried hard to remember, but I couldn't. "What do the colors of the ring have to do with anything?"

I closed my eyes and joined my eleven-year-old self inside the dank cave. It was creepy being back there. I hated small spaces, and now that I was older, the walls appeared even more constrictive. The look on her face was one of sheer terror, but I couldn't waste a moment feeling sorry for her. I had to leave before the explosion this time. I glanced down at her small, tightly clenched fist, and there they were. One red. One green. The other blue. I repeated the colors a few times because I did not want to have to go back there. As I repeated the colors, I kept my eyes riveted on her hand. My medulla oblongata—the most impressive thing I learned to say in my high school Biology class— began receiving distress messages from my heart and lungs. I turned to leave with one last fleeting glance at her frightened little face. I always left the cave regretful that I didn't know then what I knew now. I often wished I could comfort that frightened eleven-year-old girl. I wished she knew that things unfolded for her in an extraordinarily phenomenal way and what a waste it was to have lived most of her life in fear.

I opened my eyes. "Okay, so I remember the colors. What do they mean?" I asked.

I got no answer, so I went fishing. I tried every conceivable quiz-solving technique I knew but came up empty-handed. I hated trivia. I felt like that game show contestant that viewers like me screamed at from their couches for missing a subtle yet blatant clue.

I gave up pleaded, "God, please. I have no idea. What do the colors mean?"

"Red: atonement. Green: rebirth. Blue: eternal life," He said.

"What? Really?" There was no way I was hearing right. Nathan had already said what the three rings were, which made perfect sense to me. But this? This made no sense whatsoever.

I called Emma right away, but when I told her, I got an unexpected response. "Wow! That's pretty amazing," she said sounding quite awestruck.

"Wait, you understand what this means?" I asked, astonished.

"Jabez, that's the message of the Gospel," she said quite matter-of-fact.

I thought about it for a split second and gasped. "This is about Salvation?"

She chuckled. "Yeah, the order speaks to the process by which we are saved."

"Oh my God. This is so amazing! I see it now. The red is the blood of Jesus. The Bible says that God offered Jesus up as a sacrifice of atonement for our sins. The green is rebirth, being born again . . . the Bible says that if any man is in Christ, he is a new creature. And the blue? The Bible says that the gift of God is eternal life."

"Yes, that's it," Emma said. "Jabez, this is unbelievable."

"I know. You got it right away . . . and you say you don't hear God talk to you the way I do? This is totally amazing."

After I got off the phone, though, my logical brain—the part that I power down so as to be able to accept most of what happens to me—kicked in. "God, this has got to be the craziest thing You have ever revealed to me. I can't believe that you gave this to me in such an unbelievable, unimaginable way. This just blows my mind."

"What did you name your children?"

It took me all of a second to get it. My hands flew to my mouth. The meaning of the kids' actual names: spear (used to pierce Jesus' side resulting in His blood being shed), rebirth, Divine gift.

The hairs on the back of my neck stood at attention, and my body temperature plummeted. When I named each child at birth, I liked that their names had strong meanings. However, I could never in my wildest dreams fathom how strong. I thought of the role the kids played in my life, helping me to toe the line concerning God's will for my life and speaking into my life in a way no one else could. Nathan had been right. They were the three rings.

"Thank you for confirming this for me. You showed me the death and destruction after the explosion so that I could witness the wages of sin. That's why I couldn't let go of what You gave me. If I did, I too would be lost. Thank you so much for your gift to me," I said, totally humbled, tears streaming down my face.

It took me a while to compose myself. "There's still the issue of church. No matter how I tell people you called me out, I get a fight. I know what people think shouldn't matter, but I am being treated like a pariah by almost every churchgoing Believer I have told that I no longer go to church. I have only what you give me. Besides that, I have no other defense," I said, my voice peppered with despair.

"To obey is better than sacrifice," God said in a voice so still and small I wasn't certain I had heard it.

But I asked anyway. "What does that have to do with anything? That is what Samuel said to Saul. People no longer offer up sacrifices."

"People still offer up sacrifices to me."

"I don't understand." The euphoria I had been feeling moments earlier totally dissipated, giving way to frustration.

"A sacrifice is an offering meant to please and appease me. People offer sacrifices of: worship, thanksgiving, praise, joy, adoration.

However, like Cain's, some of their sacrifices are unacceptable to me. I favor obedience. To obey is better than sacrifice."

My system felt as though it was on sensory overload and was about to short-circuit. I wasn't sure I could deal with much more. Then, God urged me to open the Bible. When I did, immediately before me was an account of Jesus' response to being told that His mother and brothers wanted to talk to Him. He pointed to His disciples and said, "Here are my mother and my brothers. For whoever does the will of my Father in heaven is my brother and sister and mother" (Matthew 12:50, NIV).

I felt relieved. "But you still haven't answered my question. What is my ultimate purpose?"

"To do my will," God said.

I sighed in relief. My life made sense.

Then God told me to turn the pages of the Bible and immediately before me was an account of Jesus talking to His disciples. He said, "Blessed are the eyes that see what you see. For I tell you that many prophets and kings wanted to see what you see but did not see it, and to hear what you hear, but did not hear it" (Luke 10: 23-24, NIV).

I smiled, soaking it all in. It had been a lot to chew on and even more to swallow. But I was happy, totally satisfied. I fisted my hands, threw them high above my head, and lifted my face towards Heaven, "Woohoo!" I yelled, laughing.

* * *

Not so long ago, I stood by a window in a dream, staring at a tree that was right outside the window. It was obvious that the tree was laden with fruit, but I could not make out what they were. I squinted and peered, turning my head about, trying to get an angle. However, all I could see were the outlines of dark, slightly wrinkled fruits. "What are those?" I muttered, really frustrated.

Suddenly I felt like I was being watched and turned my head, startled to see an angel standing to my right. "The fruit is ripe," the angel said quite matter-of-factly.

Puzzled, I frowned. "What?"

Silent, the angel stared ahead, so I turned to look at the tree, and very slowly, the fruits came into focus. They were figs. They were picked and packed in short, wide, unvarnished, rustic barrels that perched on the branches of the tree. The barrels covered all surfaces of the tree, all the way to the very top. Instead of branches and leaves, the tree was branches and barrels.

"What does this mean?" I asked, flabbergasted.

When I got no reply, I turned my head. The angel had vanished.

As soon as I startled from my sleep, I cried, my heart thumping alarmingly hard and fast, "God what was that?"

His reply was succinct. "It is time for the harvest."

Acknowledgments

Thanks to "The Three Rings" for speaking into my life the way God intended. Mommy loves you.

Thanks to John Matthew Fox of Bookfox for his professional developmental editing skills. You are as wise as you are clever. Thanks for making me look at my "writings" as a book.

Thanks to my sister Emma whose uncanny eye for detail I found extremely annoying when we were growing up. Thanks for reading many modified versions of this book. Your help was priceless.

Thanks to my sister Abigail who just wouldn't let me quit. I can't wait for the day we jump off that mountain.

Thanks to my sister R.H. You have faithfully had my back and never tire of lending me your ear.

Thanks to my besties. Although we are different, we are bound by nuff love.

Thanks to my parents for the good times. I love you both.

Thanks to my niece Dani for all the encouragement and the research. You have helped bring me out of the technology dark ages . . .almost.

Thanks to my nephew Justin for the comic relief and music. I'm sure I know more Drake songs than a woman my age should.

Thanks to my sister G.H.N. for making me a *Words with Friends* junkie. Thanks for helping to keep my mind sharp . . . although I'm quite sure some of those words aren't words.

Thanks to Pastor James for his counsel. I appreciate the open line and your keeping me off the ledge.

Thanks to Jean for his encouragement. Keep the chocolate and wine coming.